T0306029

Building an Innovation Hotspot

APPROACHES AND POLICIES TO STIMULATING NEW INDUSTRY

ALICIA CAMERON

CRC Press is an imprint of the
Taylor & Francis Group, an **informa** business

This book is for Mark, Erin and my mother Patricia Cameron – forever an intellectual and the high-achieving inspiration in my life. And for anyone with a cheap idea.

A catalogue record for this book is available from the National Library of Australia.

ISBN: 9781486316977 (pbk)
ISBN: 9781486315253 (epdf)
ISBN: 9781486315260 (epub)

Published in print in Australia and New Zealand, and in all other formats throughout the world, by CSIRO Publishing.

CSIRO Publishing
Private Bag 10
Clayton South VIC 3169
Australia

Telephone: +61 3 9545 8400
Email: publishing.sales@csiro.au
Website: www.publish.csiro.au
Sign up to our email alerts: publish.csiro.au/earlyalert

Published in print only, throughout the world (except in Australia and New Zealand), by CRC Press, with ISBN 978-1-032-40724-1.

CRC Press
6000 Broken Sound Parkway NW, Suite 300, Boca Raton, FL 33487-2742
and
4 Park Square, Milton Park, Abingdon, Oxon, OX14 4RN
Website: www.routledge.com

CRC Press is an imprint of Taylor & Francis Group, LLC

Front cover: graphic by MaxartMix/Shutterstock.com

Edited by Elaine Cochrane
Cover design by Cath Pirret
Typeset by Envisage Information Technology
Index by Bruce Gillespie

CSIRO acknowledges the Traditional Owners of the lands that we live and work on across Australia and pays its respect to Elders past and present. CSIRO recognises that Aboriginal and Torres Strait Islander peoples have made and will continue to make extraordinary contributions to all aspects of Australian life including culture, economy and science. CSIRO is committed to reconciliation and demonstrating respect for Indigenous knowledge and science. The use of Western science in this publication should not be interpreted as diminishing the knowledge of plants, animals and environment from Indigenous ecological knowledge systems.

Foreword

I have known Lucy [Alicia] through my previous role as Chair of CSIRO (Australia's National Science Agency). Lucy is a member of the Insight Team at CSIRO whose task is to look at emerging megatrends in society including science and technology. They have done some groundbreaking work that is enabling a more resilient Australia. Lucy and the CSIRO Insight Team have also continued to look at how we drive greater innovation for our nation through better public policy.

Innovation is about finding new ways to do things, improving processes and systems, solving complex problems and challenges in new ways – all with the objective of delivering better outcomes. Innovation is fundamental to the creation of value – be that social, environmental or economic. Innovation is as important in our personal lives as it is to improving societies both nationally and globally. Innovation helps define some of our uniqueness as humans – our ability to create, innovate and adapt has been a defining characteristic of humanity.

If we can establish more innovative communities throughout society, we have the opportunity to improve the quality of life across education, healthcare, business etc. That is why this subject is so important. We need to have well-defined public policy that encourages innovation in all parts of our society. But it is not easy.

In my former roles as CEO of Telstra and Chair of CSIRO, and from my participation in several reviews of public policy and organisations, the question of how we become a more innovative nation has been a common theme. Some excellent work has been done across our universities, research agencies and national science and research bodies. More recently I have been involved in CRC programs and the NSW Government's plan to establish three innovation precincts. I am currently chairing one of those precincts – the Sydney Innovation and Technology Precinct – known as Tech Central.

When Lucy sent me the manuscript for *Building an Innovation Hotspot* and asked me to write a foreword, it immediately caught my attention. This is an area that requires ongoing national public policy debate, and I am always personally seeking practical answers to the complex challenges around establishing successful place-based innovation. Place-based innovation is foundational for a more prosperous nation.

Lucy's academic achievements, practical experience and excellent communication style means she is well qualified to discuss this complex topic. She has written an engaging, informative and insightful analysis on place-based innovation.

Her insights are based on a deep historic and global understanding of place-based innovation, rigorous academic analysis and practical experiences in establishing innovation areas. She has been able to combine this rigorous approach with her deep understanding of public policy including the role of governments, research and learning institutions, and the private sector. She also understands the unique role that technological advancements are playing in creating opportunities for greater innovation across all sectors of our society.

Lucy has structured her analysis around six focus areas that each play an essential part in establishing Innovation Hotspots. She includes excellent examples, drawing from a broad network of colleagues and research papers that have been written on this topic. It is a well-researched and well-structured analysis. It is both insightful and accessible while challenging many of the common misconceptions around the ingredients necessary for successful innovation areas.

Lucy has laid out a practical framework for anyone wanting to build an Innovation Hotspot with a well-articulated pathway for implementation – while recognising that innovation is always contextual. She wisely states that there is no one approach or recipe that will succeed, but she does provide the reader with the basic ingredients for a possible recipe, leaving us to choose what ingredients are required for success. Lucy has also managed to leave us room for creative license in implementation. She rightly reflects that '... *the ways in which we innovate are always changing*' – so within her structure there is room for diversity.

It is my pleasure to endorse Lucy's excellent insights into place-based innovation, something that remains fundamentally important in a virtually connected world. This book is essential reading for anyone interested in innovation and provides a significant contribution to the robust public policy required to build a more sustainable and vibrant future for Australia.

I hope you enjoy reading *Building an Innovation Hotspot* as much as I did.

David Thodey

Contents

Acknowledgements

This book contains the learnings of nearly 20 years of experience in innovation policy, and there are many, many people along the way who have profoundly influenced my thinking and who I'd like to thank.

The first people to really introduce me to regional development and the sponsors of my PhD were Drs Steve Garlick and Jim Gallagher from the then Northern Rivers Regional Research Institute, based in Lismore, New South Wales. Steve Garlick, who had decades of policy experience at a federal level, gave me a different perspective on Michael Porter's work, going against almost every other regional development enthusiast at the time. His predictions on the ill-fated Cellulose Valley cluster attempt in the Northern Rivers proved correct (see Chapter 1), along with his theories on university engagement and integrating science with existing regional industry. He also predicted the work-from-home boom of lifestyle regions a couple of decades before it really came to pass. Dr Gerard Goggin, although not an expert in innovation geography, also provided consistent support and had faith that all those long coffees discussing media theory would eventually result in a useful thesis. Thankfully they eventually did.

In 2006 I took my newly minted PhD and went to work in the then Queensland State Government Department of State Development, Trade and Innovation, first in creative industries support and then in information and communications technology (ICT) industry development and digital economy and productivity. In creative industries, Lindy Johnson worked hard to drive and embed design thinking across all industries in Queensland, while in ICT industry development, Paul Russell, Mal Lane, Katrina Watson, Greg Schossow and David Ives were colleagues and work friends who strove to upskill, attract investment and promote our home-grown innovative businesses and enterprises to build the economy of Queensland. Public servants really are the most professional and hardest-working people I know. They work hard because they are absolutely committed to serving the public, the state and the elected ministers of the day. They take the health of the economy personally. It was Janet Prowse, however, the previous head of Queensland State Archives, who suggested I apply for a Smithsonian Fellowship. I will forever be indebted to Janet for that suggestion and for the kind mentoring she showed me during those few months we worked together.

I want to thank the State of Queensland for its support for Smithsonian Fellowships, and the Smithsonian Museum for its support of visiting scholars. I'd like to acknowledge the contribution of that fellowship program to this book.

My 3 months in Washington DC in 2015–16, working with the staff at the Lemelson Center for Invention and Innovation in the bowels of the Smithsonian National Museum of American History on the Washington Mall, were a golden era of intellectualism for me. It was a blur of attending Brookings Institution lectures, visiting galleries and libraries, listening to spellbinding historian talks, staying with award-winning journalists, learning, writing and researching in iconic buildings (some of which I had special secret passage access to), touching original papers signed by Franklin Roosevelt, riding around in parks in winter and seeking out cafes that sold good coffee (Australian good). I need to thank Eric Hintz, Arthur Daemmrich and Chris Gauthier for making me feel so welcome there and putting up with my chatter and whining about American coffee.

In particular, though, I need to thank Drs Eric Hintz and Joyce Bedi, Ms Monica Smith and Professor Steven Adams for collaborating with me on this work. They have worked in the area of innovation and patent protection for decades and have deep knowledge, history and understanding of the theory and drivers of innovation and invention. It was a privilege to work with them, albeit briefly, and I hope this book does their contributions justice. I'd also like to thank Dr Daemmrich for providing comments on my previous reports and guiding my clumsy navigation of this broad field.

My recent work history has been in the digital analytics area of Australia's national science agency, CSIRO. My area of the Data61 Insight Team determines megatrends and describes possible future scenarios to help us prepare and be more resilient in the future. The shock of the COVID-19 pandemic underlined the importance of foresight and preparedness in almost all areas of our lives. It is imaginative and analytical work and I have incredibly talented colleagues there whom I am constantly in awe of: Drs Stefan Hajkowicz, Claire Naughtin, Hien Pham, Wen Wu, Alexandra Bratanova, Jessica Atherton, Emma Schleiger, Claire Mason and Caron Chen. I hope the final product can provide the basis of a new area of expertise.

Several people were helpful in contributing comments and knowledge. These include Professor Jonathan Roberts from Queensland University of Technology, Mr Andrew Terhorst, Dr Mark Bazzacco and the Honourable Paul Lucas, ex Deputy Premier of Queensland. I'd also like to thank Professor Bryan Willson from Colorado State University's Energy Institute for his comments and communications on how companies in Fort Collins are financed.

I'd also like to thank the crew at CSIRO Publishing; particularly Mark Hamilton for his sage, patient, prodding and yet forgiving steerage of this project as well as his expert editing, and Briana Melideo for her support for it in the first place. That meant everything. I'd also like to thank Meryn Scott from CSIRO Library Services for all her help at the end.

And, finally, the people I most need to thank are my husband Mark McDonell and daughter Erin. Most of the work for this manuscript was completed outside work hours, so I've spent most of my holidays and weekends over the last 7 months writing and not with them. Without a word, they picked up the domestic load and have been nothing but incredibly supportive of my time locked in my study writing with the door closed. Thank you both so much. I promise to come out now.

Introduction: Why do governments support innovation and why does everyone want another Silicon Valley?

On my first day of work in an economic development department of an Australian state government, my colleague told me, 'The whole program is about diversifying the economy and getting away from "rocks and crops". We're trying to build the industries of the future.'

'What are the industries of the future?' I asked, somewhat naively.

'They're anything with 'tech' in it, or that generate new intellectual property.' It was an impressively simple yet comprehensive explanation. 'We have nine priority sectors,' he went on to explain.

'How are we "building" them?'

'Marketing, networking, building precincts, supporting startups – there are a whole range of activities.'

'Do they work?'

'Of course, they work. Everything in government "works". Convincing Treasury they have a return on investment and they should keep funding them is the issue though. Unlike education or health, our department doesn't have recurrent funding. We have to ask Treasury for a new program budget every year, and they generally don't believe in economic development. They think it's a waste of money. What this state really needs is a self-sustaining innovative cluster like Silicon Valley.'

That initial exchange foretold the dynamics of my next 10 years in innovation policy. Policy that struggles to justify spending on interventionist government activity, that is trying to drive industry change and support local jobs through the creation of new technology. More than anything, it is seeking that mirage of a self-sustaining innovative industrial cluster of technologically advanced and world-leading firms exemplified by Silicon Valley – an innovation hotspot.

My experience in this space is also not unique. There have been many attempts around the world to build 'the next Silicon Valley'. A special Wikipedia page dedicated to technology parks lists 84 silicon 'somethings' (beach, fen, peninsula, roundabout, gorge, spa etc.) found on every continent on Earth except Antarctica (Wikipedia 2020).

This is book is about how governments and public sector advisory services globally have tackled stimulating innovation in a particular location over the last century or so, often in pursuit of building 'the next Silicon Valley'. It is about the trends influencing innovation policy and how it might change in the future. It will also highlight examples of where government actions have worked and where they haven't in terms of industry modernisation and creating new industry within a particular area. It will show how policy makers and business leaders can read the landscape to implement policy that has a better chance of powering economic growth through adoption and creation of technology over the coming decades. We can also learn from past experience in this field and imagine the future of innovation hotspots in an era that embraces technologies such as artificial intelligence, global platforms and currencies and blockchain-based smart contracts. With an understanding of the historical perspective and with an eye on the future, this book will provide readers with the information they need to become an innovation leader.

The conflict within: innovation gardening *v.* driving the agenda

In 1942, around 80 years after Charles Darwin published his great work *On the Origin of Species*, describing the processes of evolution in the biological world, an Austrian economist, Joseph Schumpeter (Fig. i.1), described a similar evolutionary process in the economic world. But instead of species, Schumpeter described the life and death of businesses and firms.

Darwin's theory proposed that biological species needed to adapt and develop new features and forms to survive in constantly changing environments. Schumpeter suggested that for businesses and firms to

Fig. i.1. Innovation economist Joseph Schumpeter 1883–1950. Image available for free publishing from the Volkswirtschaftliches Institut, Universität Freiburg, Freiburg im Breisgau, Germany.

survive in capitalist societies, they needed to have the capacity to develop or adopt new technology. New technology would allow them to outcompete their rivals, expand markets and survive. New technology would also power the creation of new firms through entrepreneurs. Firms that failed to develop or adopt new technology fast enough would be economically eclipsed in a process that paralleled survival of the fittest; what Schumpeter called *creative destruction*. Creative destruction of monopolies and inefficient firms and the rise of new and fast-growing technologically advanced firms would power local endogenous growth (economic growth from within) (Schumpeter 1942; Alcouffe and Kuhn 2004; Aghion and Festré 2017).

Schumpeter's theories are behind the economics of innovation and the anxieties of many governments that feel they need to promote innovation to remain economically competitive and thus survive. 'The innovation imperative', or 'innovate or perish', became popular terms in reports and papers encouraging governments to do more. Steering an innovative economy that is competitive and highly productive also allows governments to maintain high standards of living for their citizens and, importantly in democratic nations, popularity.

There is general agreement with Schumpeter's reasoning that innovation and the creation and adoption of new technology are key to economic survival; however, there is a constant war within many governments and in economic development literature as to how innovation is best achieved. Should governments merely create competitive market conditions for new technology to arise but leave it up to the market to steer and fund new technology? Or should governments take on considerable risk and expense in trying to steer markets and work directly with industry in on-the-ground interventions?

Members of treasury and finance departments that protect public funds often support low-spending, laissez-faire, macroeconomic or economy-wide approaches, sometimes described as 'creating the fertile ground' for industry to grow and innovate. They suggest the best way for governments to act is through a type of 'innovation gardening' that is focused on the landscape and soil conditions rather than active planting. This innovation gardening includes instituting supportive taxation regimes and regulations, reducing regulatory burdens and providing avenues for skilled immigration. It may also include instituting favourable labour laws and supportive infrastructure, and promoting research and development (R&D) budgets and intellectual property (IP) protections. These macroeconomic measures that impact the overall economy allow markets the freedom to develop without too much distortion or the need for excessive ongoing government support.

Other departments, however, such as those involved with economic development, regional development, innovation and industry portfolios, often seek to actively drive the innovation agenda and endogenous growth in a particular area or industry. These interventions focus on the actions and decisions of individuals and firms and can include assistance to certain priority sectors through business education, skills development, industry attraction, export assistance, research partnerships, organisational innovation, cluster development and regional marketing. These microeconomic measures can vary in cost, size and the length of time before the government sees any return on investment through taxation or other receipts. Like innovation itself, they are inherently costly and very risky.

Active interventionist policy and action often undergoes rigorous reviews. Treasury officials occasionally argue that the impacts of the programs are weak or sometimes even negative and that the programs can become a form of corporate welfare. Economic development officers, on the other hand, argue that deliberate government actions to promote innovation and modernisation initiatives have led to the greatest examples of accelerated economic development in the world. Examples often cited include those that saw the rapid growth and economic transition in the Asian Tiger economies (Japan, Taiwan, Hong Kong, South Korea and Singapore) or that brought certain regions out of agricultural dependence or manufacturing decline before their peers (e.g. Fort Collins (Chapter 8) or North Carolina (Chapter 1), both in the USA).

In times of rapid industry transition or change – such as a sudden drop in markets due to economic crises, resource depletion, emerging environmental constraints, large waves of migration or a sudden awareness of lowering productivity – governments are often encouraged by their constituents or the business sectors to just 'do something'. For example, if a region suddenly sees the closure of large factories, mines or other location-tied industries, governments are often asked by local businesses and representatives to step in and support employment in alternative growth industries before vicious cycles of economic depression, social unrest and disinvestment from the private sector set in.

Treasury and finance officers are usually sceptical that any of these on-the-ground measures are anything but a short-term political fix, and try to dampen the costs of programs through requesting extensive business cases, multifactor criteria analyses and program evaluation frameworks. Timeframes for evaluation are often short when very few of the proposed actions are likely to show any return on investment.

Whether to undertake the macroeconomic or microeconomic approach is a debate that will no doubt continue in the pursuit of finding the most efficient spend to create ongoing innovation and higher levels of productivity within a jurisdiction. The attraction of Silicon Valley to many in both finance and economic development areas is that it appears to be a self-sustaining cluster of wealth and technological development and requires very little government intervention at all.

Six different approaches to innovation to build an innovation hotspot

This book seeks to provide a short history of the microeconomic government spending measures that have been used to stimulate innovation and economic development at a subnational regional level. These measures are usually taken in order to build 'innovation hotspots' or to accelerate industry transition, business growth and new job creation within a defined area or industry. They generally exclude the macroeconomic national settings affecting IP protections, taxation and immigration, although these will be mentioned where relevant.

For the purposes of this book, an innovation hotspot is a town or city, state, precinct, or well-defined and connected group of regional businesses, that can be seen to be growing and innovating disproportionately faster than its peers in the same country. This can be measured in the growth in employment, market share and influence, registering IP and adopting new technologies. An innovation hotspot may also have higher comparative registrations of new businesses (startups) and entrepreneurs and attract higher levels of business investment or venture capital. There may also be a shift in local exports from commodities to more knowledge-intensive products and services.

The strategies adopted by government to stimulate innovation and develop new industries have been summarised into six areas (Fig. i.2). These have all been contributors to the successful creation of innovation and the development of new industries within particular locales and may also not have resulted in the desired outcome in other circumstances. Context has mattered.

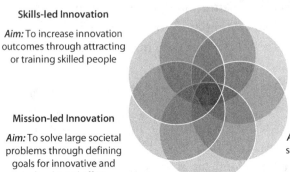

Place-led Innovation

Aim: To co-locate innovative firms and research organisations to enhance local knowledge spill-overs and improve regional branding

Skills-led Innovation

Aim: To increase innovation outcomes through attracting or training skilled people

Culture-led Innovation

Aim: To attract creative and innovative people by providing the right lifestyle and culture

Mission-led Innovation

Aim: To solve large societal problems through defining goals for innovative and technological effort

Technology-led Innovation

Aim: To modernise government services through the application of new and emerging technologies

R&D and Finance-led Innovation

Aim: To increase dedicated funding for R&D and commercialisation

Fig. i.2. Innovation strategies used by governments and organisations.

These approaches to innovation and new industry creation include innovation actions and policies that are:

- place-led
- culture-led
- technology-led
- mission-led
- finance-led
- skills-led.

These approaches are often triggered by different aims, and present different problems when used in isolation. They all seem to have gone in and out of fashion over the last century, all have their advocates and critics, and they all have been used successfully and unsuccessfully in different settings. We can learn from these experiences so that we don't keep making the same mistakes. While these innovation strategies are discussed separately in the following chapters, in many cases their application overlaps. The final chapters of this book discuss this overlap, and how a mixed-method approach can be formulated to suit the context and the place. Assessing that context and the levers available to stimulate innovation can be achieved through foresight, innovative government pivots and creating local playgrounds for experimentation and the formation of partnerships that can develop and apply technology. The final chapters will also look at how innovation itself is changing with the rapid deployment of new suites of enabling digital technologies. Artificial intelligence (AI), blockchain, the Internet of Things (IoT), augmented and virtual reality, global platforms and a new generation of robotics are fundamentally changing the way new products and services are discovered, funded, developed and applied. There is no doubt they will have a huge impact on the geography of innovation, and possibly the very definition of innovation. They will force us to deviate from our previous paths and develop new ways to capture the value of innovation within our economies.

References

Aghion P, Festré A (2017) Schumpeterian growth theory, Schumpeter, and growth policy design. *Journal of Evolutionary Economics* **27**, 25–42. doi:10.1007/s00191-016-0465-5

Alcouffe A, Kuhn T (2004) Schumpeterian endogenous growth theory and evolutionary economics. *Journal of Evolutionary Economics* **14**, 223–236. doi:10.1007/s00191-004-0205-0

Schumpeter JA (1942) *Capitalism, Socialism and Democracy.* Routledge, London and New York.

Wikipedia (2020) *List of technology centers.* <https://en.wikipedia.org/wiki/List_of_technology_centers#Places_with_%22Silicon%22_names>

1

Place-led innovation

Aim

To co-locate innovative firms and research organisations to enhance local knowledge spillovers and create or improve a regional reputation

Place-led innovation focuses on using local business dynamics and co-location to promote innovation. The rationale of many place-based efforts is that localised knowledge spillovers between similar firms or interest groups lead to accelerated innovation. Over time, this creates a critical mass of businesses within a specialised industry and the place garners a regional reputation. The regional reputation attracts further investment, and a virtuous cycle is established between investment attraction, innovation and skills development. Place-led innovation efforts by governments include creating industrial clusters, the formation of science and technology parks, regional branding, and attracting specialist industry through tax breaks, low rents and other financial incentives. Many of these efforts have been activities that seek to build 'the next Silicon Valley' or high-tech cluster.

Place-led innovation actions are incredibly seductive and attractive to political leaders because they focus on a particular jurisdiction, and they often involve media opportunities in the form of ribbon-cutting ceremonies steeped in optimism for future industries. However, place-led innovation approaches often distort natural market-led outcomes by assisting an industry to establish in a place they otherwise would not have considered. They usually also support just one type of business activity within a local centre in an attempt to create a specialised industrial cluster, sometimes at the expense of other industry opportunities.

Many place-led innovation efforts are also expensive and reap rewards only after decades of investment. They often escape investment reviews because no one wants to highlight government spending failures or lost opportunities. As Duranton (2011) states: 'Despite countless cluster initiatives and policy reports calling for cluster strategies, the economic logic behind such policies is rarely examined beyond some tautological diagrams and the mention of prosperous clusters such as the Silicon Valley.'

In many cases, place-led approaches to innovation are justified by the perceived need to correct emerging geographic inequalities in economic opportunity. The OECD, for instance, suggests that place-led innovation and enhanced productivity is essential to stabilising regions and nation-states by overcoming economic disparities:

> Since its foundation in 1999, the OECD Regional Development Policy Committee has made the case for place-based policies to help all regions use their full economic potential. Place-based policies are an indispensable complement to structural economic policies because structural economic policies do not consider specific regional factors adequately.
>
> Adopting place-based policies is particularly urgent in light of large and persistent inequalities in regional performance in many OECD countries. On average, productivity in the least productive region of a country is 46% lower than productivity in its most productive region (OECD 2019, p. 15).

The European Union is also supportive of place-led innovation efforts in the form of science and technology parks, stating that these are sound investments for public sector support (Rowe 2013).

The emergence of regional development

Place-led innovation policies began in the field of regional development that emerged during the 20th century to assist policy makers support the economic prospects of their jurisdictions (Aghion and Durlauf 2005).

Prior to the emergence of regional development as a field of study, agglomeration and industrial specialisation were seen almost as natural processes to be observed rather than steered. Business and industry clusters have formed unplanned around the world for millennia. These were sometimes formed as a result of natural or geographic features – such as the Staffordshire pottery cluster, which formed around the clay, salt, lead and coal deposits of North Staffordshire, England, or the cluster of makers of sparkling white wine in Champagne, France, which formed due to the region's ability to grow and ferment superior white grapes. Of course, port cities and large market towns also naturally developed around deep harbours or along trading routes.

The Industrial Revolution accelerated the forces of agglomeration and specialisation from the late 1700s and, as a result, many industry clusters started forming around specialist skills instead of geographic attributes. Examples of skills-based clusters include Wall Street, New York, for expertise in financial services, shares and bonds; Saville Road, London, for skilled tailors and suit-makers; and Geneva, Switzerland, for watches and clocks. There is no doubt that industrial clusters exist and form highly productive centres of industrial activity that often create world-leading products and services. These intensive industry clusters and specialisations can support entire national economies and power innovative activity.

English economist, politician and anti-protectionist David Ricardo (1772–1823) was one of the first to suggest the economic benefits of industrial specialisation and international trade (with one supporting the other) through his theory of comparative advantage (Henderson 1997). Ricardo demonstrated in a crude empirical calculation that it was advantageous to both national economies of two trading nations if industry specialised and traded freely, even if the goods of one economy were consistently cheaper than the other. Ricardo published his theory in 1817 and, 70 years later, another classical economist, Alfred Marshall (Fig. 1.1), made several observations on the advantages (and disadvantages) of industrial

Fig. 1.1. Industrial districts were first described by classical economist Alfred Marshall (1842–1922). Public domain image.

specialisation and agglomeration in his study of 'industrial districts' (Marshall 1890).

Marshall studied urbanisation and the development of specialist towns around cotton-milling, manufacturing, ceramics, finance and precision engineering before and during the early Industrial Revolution. Marshall attributed regional agglomeration and specialisation to three main forces:

1. information exchange and knowledge spillovers
2. a specialised and deep labour market
3. the upstream and downstream linkages between supply firms that a specialised local industry can provide.

He also suggested that specialised industry centres increased the convenience for customers buying specialist or expensive goods, and thus the consumers built the market. People buying would flock to the place where the best or most skilled tradespeople could be found and where they could efficiently compare products and services. The goods that people were prepared to travel for were not the domestic, everyday consumables, but the prized material possessions that would last for years or could be passed down through generations. Therefore, Marshall hypothesised, industries that dealt in expensive or luxury goods would cluster before others.

The downsides of industrial districts and single industry towns, however, included mass unemployment in economic downturns, skills shortages in sudden economic upswings, and problems related to large, unplanned, rapid urban growth, such as rent increases, poor housing and declining population health.

According to Marshall, royal houses and courts were the first to actively create clusters of skilled artisans, 'the greater part of England's manufacturing industry before the era of cotton and steam had its course directed by settlements of Flemish and other artisans; many of which were made under the immediate direction of the Plantagenet and Tudor kings' (Marshall 1890). Marshall also suggested industrial clusters would be weakened by advances in communications (such as the telephone). Better communications would allow for knowledge transfers from distant places and reduce the need for proximity. Clusters would be strengthened by the movement of people, however, who would be drawn to set up shop in specialised centres where possible.

Marshall's principles on industrial agglomeration laid the foundations for the active regional development that slowly emerged over the 20th century. Governments at all levels became more interventionist in steering business activity within their jurisdictions. Early regional development and economic development policies sought to attract new industries to certain parts of the city or region through industrial zoning and city planning, usually providing cheaper land and rents to industry. Sometimes companies were offered lower taxes to move to industrial zones. The mechanisms were relatively passive, though, and allowed market forces to do most of the heavy lifting in regard to industrial location.

The rise of science and technology parks

In 1951, Stanford University, in California, US, partnered with the City of Palo Alto's local government to create Stanford Industrial Park, later Stanford Research Park. This is often credited as being the first science and technology park (STP), along with seeding the high-tech research cluster that became Silicon Valley (Sandelin 2006; UNESCO 2017). Information and communications technology (ICT) firms Hewlett-Packard and Varian were two of the first tenants at Stanford Research Park.

While Stanford Research Park contributed to the growth of Silicon Valley, some suggest it played only a minor part in its development and that Silicon Valley's origins date to half a century before Stanford Research Park was developed. Entrepreneurial engineering and technology firms began establishing around the San Francisco Bay area in the early 1900s and took advantage of naval and military contracts for radio and electronics before and during the First and Second world wars – long before the development of Stanford Research Park (Hintz 2015; Adams *et al.* 2018); also see Chapter 6.

After the apparent success of Stanford Research Park, technology parks were established along Boston's Route 128 (1955) and in North Carolina's Research Triangle (1959), both also in the US.

Boston's Route 128 had the pre-existing world-leading research institutions of Harvard University and Massachusetts Institute of Technology (MIT) and evolved somewhat organically with help from regional marketing campaigns to attract other technology companies. In contrast, North Carolina's Research Triangle was the product of a very deliberate and coordinated effort by government bodies and three universities (North Carolina State University, Duke University, and University of North Carolina at Chapel Hill) which made up 'The Triangle' to bring in specialist high-tech industries and manufacturing to the state. The aim was to boost state income, increase the GDP per capita and move the primary industry of North Carolina away from its agricultural base.

> Silicon Valley, Boston's Route 128 and Research Triangle Park are three of the most well-known clusters in the United States and among those most often associated with entrepreneurship and innovation. However, the role of public policy in creating and sustaining these regions as attractive locations for entrepreneurship is complex.

Interestingly, while Silicon Valley and Route 128 certainly benefited from federal research funds, neither arose as a result of a cohesive or academic institution. On the other hand, the Research Triangle Park in North Carolina was clearly a product of dedicated state-level planning (Chatterji *et al.* 2014).

Other early examples of successful STPs that followed Stanford Research Park include Tsukuba Science City in Japan (created in the 1960s), Daejeon region's Daedeok Innopolis in South Korea (created in the early 1970s) and Cambridge Science Park in the UK (Fig. 1.2). Tsukuba Science City and the Daejeon Daedeok Innopolis were a result of state-level planning to concentrate research and development (R&D) efforts of several large public sector organisations in one place, while Cambridge Science Park, created in 1970, was attached to the existing globally recognised Cambridge University and sought to enhance the commercialisation outcomes of research being done in the university.

Fig. 1.2. Cambridge Science Park. 'Cambridge Science Park new Napp Pharmaceutical Group buildings in April 2011' by cmglee is licenced under CC BY-SA 3.0.

Cambridge Research Park is now credited as playing a 'pivotal role' in creating 'the Cambridge phenomenon', the moniker now given to the rapid growth of high-tech startups in the Cambridge area that make it 'one of the leading technology hotspots in the world' (Cambridge Science Park 2020).

These early success stories led to a rapid rise in the establishment of STPs around the world, particularly from the 1980s onwards. In the US, the establishment of STPs peaked in 1984 and again in 2005 before dropping away sharply in the 2010s (Hobbs *et al.* 2017). Between 1951 and 2015 there were 146 STPs established in the US alone.

Michael E Porter and why everyone wants to build a cluster

Place-led innovation efforts gained a boost after the publication of the highly influential book *The Competitive Advantage of Nations* by Harvard Professor Michael E Porter in 1990 (Porter 1990) (Fig. 1.3). The book, along with a series of *Harvard Business Review* articles issued shortly after, became one of the most highly cited texts in government policy documents concerning regional development and economic development over the next two decades (Aktouf *et al.* 2005; Huggins and Izushi 2011; Swords 2013).

Fig. 1.3. Harvard Professor Michael E Porter. Photo by Cmproject is licenced under CC BY-SA 4.0.

Porter collected evidence from 10 nations on specialised industrial clusters. His results suggested that national competitive advantage is enhanced by, and increasingly dependent on, the development of these specialised industrial clusters co-located in dynamic and highly innovative locales. Porter produced a 'diamond' diagram that suggested national competitive advantage gained by industrial clusters was derived from the interplay between:

1. firm strategy, structure and rivalry
2. demand conditions
3. related supporting industries
4. factor conditions (land, labour, natural resources, capital and infrastructure).

> Geographic, cultural, and institutional proximity leads to special access, closer relationships, better information, powerful incentives, and other advantages in productivity and innovation that are difficult to tap from a distance. The more the world economy becomes complex, knowledge-based, and dynamic, the more this is true (Porter 1998).

Porter's work emphasised the importance of immediate place in driving innovation, specialisation and productivity, leading to the creation of new industries and therefore improving national productivity and competitiveness.

Although Porter specifically warned against government actions that took a 'pre-eminent role' in cluster development, many policy documents that cite Porter's work use it to justify direct government support for targeted industry interventions to deliberately build clusters (Swords 2013). The emphasis on local geography in supporting innovative clusters provides the ammunition many policy makers need to support place-led innovation policies, particularly when taking their proposals for action to their treasury officials. As Brakman and van Marrewijk (2013) state:

> policies that support your location or stimulate your sector have always been in demand. When combined with the

overwhelming empirical evidence that higher density is associated with higher productivity, this demand makes it easier to justify cluster policies.

In addition to Porter, other theorists, such as David Audretsch (1996), also published influential work on the importance of proximity in knowledge spillovers to new knowledge industries and job creation, particularly with the rise in importance of small and medium-sized enterprises (SMEs).

Clusters and the enslaved in a digital age: technopoles and the work of Manuel Castells

Michael E Porter's work was published alongside the widespread take-up of personal computers in the 1980s and early 1990s, but before the general deployment of the internet. Although Porter thought an increasingly globalised world would concentrate knowledge in small specialist centres, sociologist Manuel Castells was one of the first to describe the geographic impact of the internet on industry and innovation. He used the term 'technopole' to describe a world-leading cluster of firms in ICT development – such as Silicon Valley.

As a sociologist, Castells was particularly interested in the power relationships new technology-enabled technopoles would create. A technopole would command authority and control over lesser regions by concentrating the power, data intelligence and overt and covert decision-making that could be done by new online businesses and data analytics firms. In his books *Technopoles of the World: The Making of 21st Century Industrial Complexes* (Castells and Hall 1994) and *The Rise of the Network Society* (Castells 2000), Castells describes changing power relationships between regions as a result of online technologies. This, in turn, fed the anxieties of some policy makers that unless their region developed a world-leading ICT-based technopole they risked being left behind or, worse, enslaved, by high-technology centres in other parts of the world.

Cluster-theory in the 2020s

There is no doubt that industrial clusters are highly productive and innovative and can disproportionately contribute to the growth and development of national economies (Delgado *et al.* 2014). The level of productivity and innovation benefits derived from physical co-location can be affected by several factors, including how much R&D is undertaken by firms in the clusters, the type of core industry in the cluster, how specialised the cluster has become, and whether it trades externally or just to nearby regional businesses (Mo *et al.* 2020). The anchoring tenants of the cluster also impact its performance: whether they are state-centred (R&D institutions of government departments), nodes of multinational companies (a satellite platform cluster), locally grown with external branches (hub and spoke model) or large suppliers of regional businesses (Marshallian) (Markusen 1996; He and Fallah 2011). Clusters with high levels of patenting and employment have also been shown spawn new industries, and clusters that build on existing strengths are more effective than those that do not (Delgado *et al.* 2014).

Recent developments in digital technologies and innovation methodologies are challenging these cluster typographies. Digital twins, videoconferencing and virtual/augmented reality will change the dynamics and benefits of co-location. External and enabling capacity via digital networks may reduce the benefits of co-location between like firms, or between firms that complement or enable each other. The development of digital or virtual hubs may also reduce the need for physical co-location and enable far greater levels of open innovation (Ashmore *et al.* 2019) (see Chapters 3 and 7), although the impacts of digital technologies on cluster development in the post-COVID era are yet to be fully studied.

The problems with place-led innovation efforts: they are very expensive and not all succeed

Co-location efforts to build clusters are hugely expensive and take decades to produce results. To build and attract enough industry to fill a technology park, for instance, is no small feat, and not every research institution or government attempt succeeds. Of the hundreds of attempts to replicate Silicon Valley (87 according to one list [Wikipedia 2021]), very few have grown to be successful, highly innovative centres of world-leading industry and development. The World Bank (2010c) states: 'Technology and science parks are favoured by policy makers, as they make innovation efforts highly visible. Experience shows, however, that few are successful.'

Vivek Wadhwa from Carnegie Mellon's School of Engineering at Silicon Valley is even more scathing:

> Porter and legions of consultants following his methodology prescribed top-down clusters to governments all over the world. The formula was always the same: select a hot industry, build a science park next to a research university, provide subsidies and incentives for chosen industries to locate there, and create a pool of venture capital.
>
> Sadly, the magic never happened – anywhere. Hundreds of regions all over the world collectively spent tens of billions of dollars trying to build their versions of Silicon Valley. I don't know of a single success (Wadhwa 2013).

Due to the number of failed attempts and costly false starts, a growing number of researchers have attempted to isolate the factors that create successful technology parks (Link and Scott 2000; Link 2002; Al-Kfairy *et al.* 2019; Ferreira de Faria *et al.* 2019; Link 2019).

Margaret Pugh O'Mara (2005), in her influential book *Cities of Knowledge* (2005), outlines the development of R&D hubs around regional universities in the US in the 20th century, but particularly in the post-war period. She suggests there are four take-home lessons that policy makers should consider if trying to build 'the next Silicon Valley':

> you need a lot of money, you need a powerful university, you need control of land in the right location, in particular, large parcels of land in locations desirable to middle-class professionals, and you need to make high-tech development the end, not the means (Pugh O'Mara 2005).

Pugh O'Mara strongly suggests that successful 'knowledge cities' are focused on the science rather than the desire to 'save the city'.

Luger and Goldstein (1991) make a similar list of conditions necessary for research park success, but with additions that include transport infrastructure and business networks, such as a good airport, forward-thinking, effective political and business leaders, and universities that include medical schools and engineering institutes. Pugh O'Mara and Luger and Goldstein saw the size and research reputation of a university attached to a science park as central to its ability to make products, patent technology, attract funds and commercialise research. A good research reputation is critical to its ability to attract the physical presence of private enterprise.

While there is no doubt that high technology clusters are some of the most productive areas in the world, the role of government in building them is less clear. One of the reasons why the World Bank, for instance, may favour macroeconomic approaches before large investments in STPs or expensive clustering efforts is that STPs are risky and need large sums of ongoing funding, often at the expense of broader education programs.

The World Bank's approach is somewhat supported by Chatterji *et al.* (2014), who examined factors associated with entrepreneurship, a critical element to building clusters. They suggested that macroeconomic policies to increase skilled migration, strengthen the education systems to build the pool of local (not imported) entrepreneurs and startups and eliminate unwise or restrictive regulation would do more to help local innovation than other specific clustering actions:

> Even though entrepreneurship is a powerful force that engenders local and economic growth, it is not obvious that government policy can create entrepreneurship. Even if entrepreneurs naturally cluster in tight geographic units, it is not obvious that governments should use public policy to support such clusters (Chatterji *et al.* 2014).

Table 1.1. Advantages and disadvantages of place-led innovation efforts

Advantages	Disadvantages
• Can build a regional reputation for a particular industry. This, in turn, may attract investment and increase migration of skilled labour and growth of new enterprises. • Can facilitate knowledge spillovers between firms and businesses and thus increase highly valuable informal networks of learning and opportunity. • Can build local supply chains and supportive or associated specialist industries. For example, along with the specialist industry it may build industry-specific education, banking, insurance and finance sectors. • Can incentivise long-term knowledge intensification and innovation systems within a jurisdiction. This may reduce dependence on commodity products or improve local education levels and, in turn, increase incomes and future prospects of the broader local economy.	• Expensive and long-term. Building industry clusters, science and technology parks and knowledge-intensive systems is no short-term or simple process. Many attempts have failed. Industry clusters generally take decades to grow and may draw heavily on state finances while they do so. This may be at the expense of other broader-based business or education programs. • Interferes with the market. The decision to locate a business is usually a commercial one. If businesses are incentivised by government to locate in a particular place, they may not stay there once the incentives run out, or they may damage their own commercial prospects by moving to a suboptimal operating environment. • Makes a place susceptible to downturns in a single industry. Industry clusters or single-industry towns sometime come at the expense of a diversified economy. Diversified economies may be more resilient in turbulent economic conditions such as global downturns or times of conflict. • May create skills shortages in times of rapid growth. An industry cluster creates high demand for specialist skills and, in times of rapid market expansion, this can create skills shortages and lead to rapid increases in wages. This also puts pressure on local education systems to keep up.

Successful place-led innovation – Research Triangle, North Carolina

The Research Triangle Park in Raleigh–Durham–Chapel Hill, North Carolina, is the largest research park in the US. It was negotiated in the 1950s in a deliberate effort by local governments and existing universities to transform the industrial landscape of North Carolina, create new industries and attract R&D institutions and the innovation laboratories of private companies.

In the 1950s, the state of North Carolina had one of the lowest incomes per capita in the US. Industry was largely dependent on tobacco, textiles and furniture manufacturing. The research capacity at the three resident

Fig. 1.4.   Postcard of North Carolina 'Research Triangle Park' *c.* 1960s. State Archives of North Carolina.

universities (University of North Carolina at Chapel Hill, Duke University, and North Carolina State University) was seen by state politicians as a tool for economic development, particularly after witnessing the rise of industry in Silicon Valley and Boston's industrial precinct of Route 128 (see Chapter 2).

State politicians acted with members of the three universities to create a not-for-profit corporation (Research Triangle Institute) to acquire disused agricultural land between the three universities. Research Triangle Institute operated under separate management with separate facilities, staff and board of governors, but contained representatives from all three universities and the state.

Formally created in 1959 and covering over 2800 ha, the North Carolina Research Triangle Park now accommodates over 300 companies employing over 55 000 employees (Fig. 1.4) (North Carolina History Project 2015). In 2019 it ranked fourth in the US for skills attraction after San Francisco Bay Area, Seattle and Washington–Baltimore (Kerr 2019).

The North Carolina Research Triangle is known for its steady and sustained effort in creating the high-tech research cluster over the last 60 years. It is also credited with transforming the local economy from having one of the lowest incomes per capita, based on seasonal agricultural produce, to one of the highest, based on skilled jobs and high-tech industry.

Research Triangle Park was a critical factor in transforming North Carolina from the nation's second poorest state in 1959 to one of the fastest growing biotechnology clusters in the country, and the third largest biotechnology cluster in the Western hemisphere, after California and Massachusetts (Cummings 2020).

It should be noted that early and long-term federal government tenancies in the North Carolina Research Triangle Park were substantial, and possibly critical to its development. Two large federal government research laboratories – those of the Environmental Protection Agency and the National Institutes of Health – were attracted to the park within the first few years. Each of these laboratories brought in tenured waged staff, and multi-million-dollar budgets for research on national priorities.

The federal laboratories and university facilities were complemented by early private investment. R&D laboratories for computer giant IBM located to the park within 5 years, and an average of six biotechnology companies per year were attracted to the park since its development (North Carolina History Project 2015).

Where place-led innovation didn't achieve its aims – Cellulose Valley Technology Park, Lismore, Australia

On 16 June 2000, the local member for Northern Rivers in the New South Wales parliament, the Honourable Harry Woods MP, announced that Southern Cross University would receive a $1 million government grant to develop 'Cellulose Valley Technology Park'. Cellulose Valley Technology Park was to be a 73-ha park adjacent to the small, regional university that would be developed in 'close association with Australia's leading companies with an involvement in natural and complementary products'.

In a region best known for its counterculture, alternative lifestyles and stunning geography, Cellulose Valley Technology Park would build on local industry strengths in natural plant-based supplements and herbal remedies. Local firms with a global market for products based on tea tree oil (Fig. 1.5), echinacea supplements and other herbal remedies could have the medicinal properties tested by clinicians from the natural health and science faculty at Southern Cross University, and then use the results in growing and commercialising their products and firms. As the Pro-Vice Chancellor of Research, Professor Peter Baverstock, put it, 'creating synergies between scientists and researchers, manufacturers, primary producers, regulators, and of course, practitioners of herbal medicine' (Baer 2016).

It was hoped that, in the first year of operation, large and well-known firms in natural medicines, supplements and products would have a presence at the park (eight companies had expressed an interest in being located there), and then slowly build their manufacturing facilities, supporting the university, the

Fig. 1.5. *Melaleuca alternifolia* flowers, from the Australian tree that produces the antifungal tea tree oil. Csubbra, CC BY-SA 3.0 <https://creativecommons.org/licenses/by-sa/3.0>, via Wikimedia Commons.

region, and innovation in the use of natural plant products and their applications (Mattar 2008). It was projected that the park would create over 1000 direct jobs in the following 10 years (Hyland 1999).

It seems that only half of the secured $1 million in grant money was paid and those funds secured the land for the park, paid for two coordinating staff and built a road (Southern Cross University 2002). Unfortunately, after 3 years the park still had no residents. Local firms did not see the benefit in moving to the Cellulose Valley Technology Park as they could still sponsor clinical trials or pay Southern Cross University (or indeed other universities with a higher profile) to test their products while being located elsewhere.

Firms from outside the area were not incentivised by the university linkages or the facilities to outlay the considerable expense to move into the park. The idea of Cellulose Valley Technology Park was slowly shelved and plans for the park quietly disappeared from the university website.

Summary

There is no doubt that successful industrial clusters are highly productive, inspirational centres of industry and innovation, particularly in knowledge-intensive industries. Place-based efforts to build industrial clusters have often focused narrowly on co-locating firms into defined districts or science and technology parks attached to universities. This approach used on its own is expensive, takes a long time and has a high failure rate. The popularity of intense cluster-building peaked after Michael Porter's influential books and papers on the subject were published in the 1980s and 1990s but has since declined as the long-term expense of sustaining artificially created clusters has proven too great for many shorter-term governments. A hotspot is a place-based effort, however, and the coming chapters will cover the other aspects of place-building that incentivise clusters to form more organically.

References

Adams SB, Chambers D, Schultz M (2018) A moving target: the geographic evolution of Silicon Valley, 1953–1990. *Business History* **60**, 859–883. doi:10.1080/00076791.2017.1346612

Aghion P, Durlauf SN (2005) *Handbook of economic growth. Volume 1A.* Elsevier, Amsterdam; Boston.

Aktouf O, Chenoufi M, Holford WD (2005) The false expectations of Michael Porter's strategic management framework. *Problems and Perspectives in Management* **3**, 181–200.

Al-Kfairy M, Khaddaj S, Mellor RB (2019) Computer modelling and identification of factors important for the success of business clusters. *International Journal of Knowledge-based Development* **10**, 384–405. doi:10.1504/IJKBD.2019.105114

Ashmore F, Price L, Deville J (2019) Be Bold. Be Innovative. Be a Digital Hub, A CORA Project Report. University of Lincoln, Lincoln.

Audretsch DB (1996) Innovative clusters and the industry life cycle. *Review of Industrial Organization* **11**, 253–273.

Baer H (2016) *Complementary Medicine in Australia and New Zealand: Its popularisation, legitimation and dilemmas.* Routledge, New York

Brakman S, van Marrewijk C (2013) Reflections on cluster policies. *Cambridge Journal of Regions, Economy and Society* **6**, 217–231. doi:10.1093/cjres/rst001

Cambridge Science Park (2020) *Where technologies thrive.* Cambridge Science Park, Cambridge. <https://www.cambridgesciencepark.co.uk/about-park/>

Castells M (2000) *The Rise of the Network Society.* 2nd edn. Blackwell Publishers, Oxford; Malden, Mass.

Castells M, Hall P (1994) *Technopoles of the World: The making of twenty-first-century industrial complexes.* Routledge, London and New York.

Chatterji A, Glaeser E, Kerr W (2014) Clusters of entrepreneurship and innovation. *Innovation Policy and the Economy* **14**, 129–166. doi:10.1086/674023.

Cummings A (2020) *Brain Magnet: Research Triangle Park and the idea of the idea economy*. Columbia University Press, New York.

Delgado M, Porter ME, Stern S (2014) Clusters, convergence, and economic performance. *Research Policy* **43**, 1785–1799. doi:10.1016/j.respol.2014.05.007

Duranton G (2011) California dreamin': the feeble case for cluster policies. *Review of Economic Analysis* **3**, 3–45.

Ferreira de Faria A, de Almeida Ribeiro J, Gonçalves do Amaral MG, Sedyama JAS (2019) Success factors and boundary conditions for technology parks in the light of the triple helix model. *Journal of Business and Economics* **10**, 50–67. doi:10.15341/jbe(2155-7950)/01.10.2019/005

He J, Fallah MH (2011) The typology of technology clusters and its evolution – evidence from the hi-tech industries. *Technological Forecasting and Social Change* **78**, 945–952. doi:10.1016/j.techfore.2011.01.005

Henderson JP (1997) *The Life and Economics of David Ricardo*. Springer US, Boston, MA.

Hintz E (2015) Suburban garage hackers + lab researchers = personal computing. In *Places of Invention*. (Eds AP Molella, A Karvellas) pp. 14–41. Smithsonian Institution Scholarly Press, Washington DC.

Hobbs KG, Link AN, Scott JT (2017) The growth of US science and technology parks: does proximity to a university matter? *The Annals of Regional Science* **59**, 495–511. doi:10.1007/s00168-017-0842-5

Huggins R, Izushi H (2011) *Competition, Competitive Advantage, and Clusters: The Ideas of Michael Porter*. Oxford Scholarship Online. doi:10.1093/acprof:oso/9780199578030.003.0001

Hyland H (1999) Southern Cross University Submission to the inquiry into infrastructure and the development of Australia's regional areas. Standing Committee on Primary Industries and Regional Services. Australian Parliament House, Canberra, Australia.

Kerr WR (2019) *The Gift of Global Talent: How migration shapes business, economy & society*. Stanford Business Books, Stanford, California.

Link AN (2019) University science and technology parks: A US perspective. In *Science and Technology Parks and Regional Economic Development*. (Eds S Amoroso, AN Link and M Wright) pp. 25–38. Palgrave Macmillan, Greensboro, NC.

Link AN (2002) *From Seed to Harvest: The growth of the Research Triangle Park*. Research Triangle Foundation of North Carolina, Research Triangle Park, North Carolina.

Link AN, Scott JT (2000) *The Growth of Research Triangle Park*. University of North Carolina at Greensboro and Dartmouth College, Greensboro, NC and Hanover, NH.

Luger MI, Goldstein HA (1991) *Technology in the Garden: Research parks and regional economic development.* University of North Carolina Press, Chapel Hill.

Markusen A (1996) Sticky places in slippery space: a typology of industrial districts. *Economic Geography* **72**, 293–313. doi:10.2307/144402

Marshall A (1890) *The Principles of Economics.* Macmillan, London.

Mattar Y (2008) Post-industrialism and Silicon Valley as models of industrial governance in Australian public policy. *Telematics and Informatics* **25**, 246–261. doi:10.1016/j.tele.2007.04.001

Mo C, He C, Yang L (2020) Structural characteristics of industrial clusters and regional innovation. *Economics Letters* **188**, 109003. doi:10.1016/j.econlet.2020.109003

North Carolina History Project (2015) *Research Triangle Park.* <http://northcarolinahistory.org/encyclopedia/research-triangle-park/>

OECD (2019) *Regional Outlook 2019: Leveraging megatrends for cities and rural areas.* OECD, Paris, France. <https://www.oecd-ilibrary.org/content/publication/9789264312838-en>

Porter ME (1990) *The Competitive Advantage of Nations.* Collier Macmillan, London.

Porter ME (1998) POLICY: Clusters and the new economics of competition. *Harvard Business Review* **76**, 77–90.

Rowe D (2013) Setting up, managing and evaluating EU science and technology parks: An advice and guidance report on good practice. European Commission, Luxembourg.

Sandelin J (2006) *Co-Evolution of Stanford University & the Silicon Valley: 1950 to today.* WIPO, New York.

Southern Cross University (2002) Annual Report. Southern Cross University, Lismore, Australia.

Swords J (2013) Michael Porter's cluster theory as a local and regional development tool: the rise and fall of cluster policy in the UK. *Local Economy* **28**, 369–383. doi:10.1177/0269094213475855

UNESCO (2017) Science Policy and Capacity Building; Science and Technology Park Governance: Concept and Definition. UNESCO, Paris.

Wadhwa V (2013) Silicon Valley can't be copied. MIT Technology Review. MIT Technology Review, Boston.

Wikipedia (2021) *List of technology centers.* <https://en.wikipedia.org/wiki/List_of_technology_centers#Places_with_%22Silicon%22_names>

World Bank (2010) Innovation Policy: A Guide for Developing Countries. World Bank, Washington DC.

2

Culture-led innovation

Aim

To attract creative and innovative people by providing the right lifestyle and culture

What sort of lifestyle do creative young tech entrepreneurs want? How can we attract and support emerging entrepreneurs with the will and knowledge to build new businesses? These questions were suddenly front-of-mind for urban planners, regional developers and policy makers in the late 1990s and early 2000s after the publication of two blockbuster books that focused attention on the role of local culture in innovation and the development of new industries. These books were *Regional Advantage: Culture and Competition in Silicon Valley and Route 128* by political scientist and economist Professor AnnaLee Saxenian (Saxenian 1996) and *The Rise of the Creative Class* by urban geographer Richard Florida (Florida 2003).

Regional Advantage

In *Regional Advantage*, AnnaLee Saxenian (Fig. 2.1) compared the fortunes of Boston's Route 128 on the East Coast of the US with Silicon Valley on the West Coast from the late 1950s onwards. These two areas had similar economic profiles in the 1950s and faced similar global challenges, but their fortunes diverged radically in the early 1980s. Silicon Valley emerged to be the largest information and communications technology (ICT) cluster in the world, while Boston's Route 128 stumbled in the face of emerging global competition.

Fig. 2.1. UC Berkeley Professor AnnaLee Saxenian. 'Photograph of AnnaLee Saxenian, speaker at 'Moore's Law at 40 Symposium', 12–13 May 2005, organised by the Chemical Heritage Foundation' by Science History Institute is licenced under CC BY-SA 3.0.

From the late 1950s to the early 1970s, both Silicon Valley and Boston's Route 128 were thriving and promising centres for semiconductors, electronics and personal computing equipment and software. Both areas had:

- existing world-leading research institutions – Silicon Valley had Stanford University while Route 128 had Massachusetts Institute of Technology (MIT) and Harvard University
- benefited from large defence contracts during the Second World War and then post-war spending for electronics
- a similar sized workforce and skills mix.

In the early 1970s, both areas were seen as the future of American industry, especially as other traditional manufacturing areas that focused on cars and white goods had started to fall into decline. In the early 1980s, however, both Route 128 and Silicon Valley faced an existential threat from Japanese and Korean manufacturers, similar to the threat that faced the American car industry. As Silicon Valley started to move away from invention and into mass-production of ICT products, they began to compete directly with newly developed semiconductor and personal computing firms in Japan and South Korea. Making higher quality and cheaper computing parts than many

US-based firms, these countries started taking global market share away from US-based firms and analysts predicted that – like the car manufacturing centre of Detroit and steelworks of Pittsburgh – Silicon Valley and Route 128 would be heading into decades of slow decline in the face of increased global competition.

ICT companies located in Route 128, Massachusetts, began to shrink in the face of this threat, and many large companies began to downsize their workforces. Industry in Silicon Valley, however, continued to grow. Silicon Valley firms adapted rapidly to the global competition and a new breed of startups, including Apple, Microsoft and Sun Microsystems, created a new generation of computing products. These both supplemented and supported the older firms such as Intel and Hewlett-Packard (HP). Since that time, Silicon Valley has grown to be the largest centre of global innovation in computing in the world while Boston 128 – while still innovative – grew comparatively more slowly and is now a much smaller centre of technology activity, along with other rising areas such as New York and North Carolina on the East Coast.

By 1996, when Saxenian's book was published, Silicon Valley had dwarfed Route 128 in market capital, exports, number of fast-growing companies, venture capital and skilled workforce. What was the difference? Why did one area suddenly thrive while the other stumbled? Saxenian attributes the divergent fortunes to the local culture and the fundamentally different industrial ecosystems and productive organisation.

Different cultures lead to difference responses to competition

In the post-war period of the 1950s–1970s, Silicon Valley's business and tech community was small but highly networked and they worked and played together. Many in that network were ex-Stanford University students who had studied engineering under Professor Fred Terman. Terman had encouraged his former students to start businesses and win federal defence contracts. Through regular and supportive business assistance, Terman created familiar networks with the budding entrepreneurs in the emerging electronics industry. Members of this highly networked group were often formerly from the mid-west. At Stanford they were away from their families in an open environment of development and experimentation. They were allowed to fail without damaging their reputations. They also felt freed from the oppressive East Coast institutional culture, and thus were attracted by, and became part of, the counterculture and sunny lifestyle of the San Francisco Bay Area. Computer clubs formed in homes and bars around the university, and people would swap information and equipment to create new instruments, cobbling together new machines from parts bought from the many component manufacturers. These clubs and swap events further reinforced networks of expertise and job mobility between companies.

In comparison, the Boston Route 128 area had Puritan roots, with large and powerful well-established families that went back generations. Failure at any stage of life was severely frowned upon and the social groups that formed around sporting clubs, churches, schools, universities and work institutions were far more closed, conservative and formal. After-work life was stifled by people living in the suburbs, away from their place of employment. The opportunity for development of a counterculture was limited, although a small group of hackers did emerge around Technology Square in Cambridge at the heart of the Massachusetts Institute of Technology (MIT). For the majority of workers in the Route 128 cluster, however, there was limited out-of-institution sharing of information related to their work or study, and company loyalty was highly valued. A good career involved steadily moving up the company ladder and only changing jobs to a higher level in another respected large company. Entrepreneurship was limited, and people didn't dare leave their corporate positions to risk starting companies of their own, particularly as company intellectual property (IP) was heavily legally protected. The large ICT firms along Route 128 were also often siloed and vertically integrated. They had established supply chains and it was hard for startups to get a foothold in the market.

As the ICT industry globalised from the late 1960s and the US industry moved into the mass production of components, the tightly knit community of developers and business people in Silicon Valley stayed ahead of overseas developments, and sometimes used overseas manufacturing facilities, while the East Coast companies in Route 128 were caught invested with inflexible systems and large outdated factories.

> Understanding regional economies as industrial systems rather than as clusters of factors of production, and thinking of the two regions as examples of the two models of industrial systems – the decentralized regional network-based system and the independent firm-based system – illuminates the divergent trajectories of the Silicon Valley and Route 128 economies since World War II (Saxenian 1996).

Saxenian was one of the first to starkly illustrate the role of organisational and local culture and regional networks in shaping the processes of regional innovation and innovative capacity. It was much more than business dress versus casual attire, than suits and leather shoes versus jeans, sneakers and hoodies; it was the horizontal *v.* hierarchical structures of the entire industrial system that made one more accessible and adaptable, and the other more rigid, siloed and susceptible to disruption and change.

The Rise of the Creative Class

Florida's book *The Rise of the Creative Class*, published just 2 years after Saxenian's *Regional Advantage*, sought to identify the powerful emergence of a new and increasingly valuable class – the creative class.

The creative class described by Florida was the highest order of knowledge workers across all fields – science, technology, the arts, media and the professions. This was the class of workers who created change, built wealth and designed new products and services; the class who valued autonomy because they did things differently and, in doing so, built new markets and added the most value to any organisation. These were the workers who could not be automated.

Florida used data from the US Bureau of Statistics to show that over the last century the proportion of creative workers had grown steadily

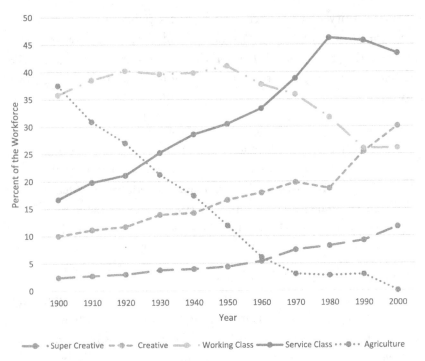

Fig. 2.2. The class structure, 1900–1999 (percentage of workforce) from *The Rise of the Creative Class*, Florida (2003) p. 75.

to comprise up to 30% of the total workforce in 2000. In doing so they were greater in number than those in the working and agricultural classes, but fewer than people working in service industries (Fig. 2.2).

Florida also described the environments where the creative class clustered: urban, diverse, tolerant, artistic, open, and technophilic. Florida suggested that suburban science and technology parks (STPs) and large corporations requiring 'organisational men' were on their way out because they had become associated with boring, isolated, mechanical lives with little social interaction. If you wanted to attract creative people, you needed to provide them with stimulating environments.

Florida extolled the attractions of inner-city urban areas (often left crumbling during the 'white flight' suburbanisation of US cities in the 1950 and 1960s) where there were high levels of social interaction, after-hours entertainment, arts that appealed to the young such as live music venues, theatres and comedy clubs, and markets thick with small enterprises. Controversially, Florida suggested that a visible gay presence highlighted open-mindedness and self-expression in a city, and that this was highly associated with rapidly rising house prices and the growth of high-tech industry.

According to Florida, creative people were attracted to environments where mastery, merit and talent mattered and were appreciated over looks, background, wealth, sexuality, status or birthright. Critically, creative people valued freedom of expression and openness. Florida backed up his theory with several empirical associations of regional wealth, job growth and innovation, entrepreneurship, and demographics and culture in the US over the previous 100 years.

Florida suggested that the secret to building vibrant and innovative locations lay not in attracting big companies through tax breaks, cheap land and other government handouts, but rather in building the social and cultural environment, the 'people climate', that could attract the diverse human talents that drive prosperity. Urban planners and policy makers should concentrate on the three Ts: technology, talent and tolerance.

Florida's next book, *The Flight of the Creative Class* (Florida 2005), argued that economic growth and competitiveness result from the attraction of talent on a global scale. Creative people are more globally mobile than in the past and are now concentrating in around 20–25 megaregions. Over the last 100 years the US has acted as an 'IQ magnet' and attracted smart creatives due to its openness and democratic values:

> Of critical importance to American success in this last century has been a tremendous influx of global talent. These were powerhouse entrepreneurs and industry builders who moulded every facet of American life, from steel titan Andrew Carnegie to financial wizard August Belmont to investor and mega philanthropist, George Soros (Florida 2005, p. 5).

The power of the US to attract creative talent was strong in the 20th century due to its being a safe haven and refuge to those fleeing fascist regimes, the world wars and other conflicts, but Florida claims this magnetic power is now waning. Smaller globally connected centres in lifestyle locations in Canada, New Zealand, Australia, Ireland and Scandinavia were increasingly pulling the global creative elite away, and doing so to build wealth and power their own economies. This was causing the 'flight' of the creative class.

> No longer will economic might amass in countries according to their natural resources, manufacturing, excellence, military dominance or even scientific and technological prowess. Today, the terms of competition revolve around a central axis: a nation's ability to mobilize, attract and retain human creative talent (Florida 2005, p. 3).

This flight is now being facilitated by better communications networks and access to high-powered computing, allowing employees to 'work from anywhere'. Liveability, security, creative opportunity, and community are the key elements to the formation of creative clusters.

Innovation and democracy

The relationship between creativity, freedom of expression, openness and innovation is often assumed, and this sometimes extends to further assumptions about the links between democracy and innovation. Increasing levels of economic development and the goal of many countries to become a technology creator (and thus become an innovation-led economy) are often viewed as stages of democratic as well as economic development. Rapidly rising innovation levels in countries such as China, Singapore and Russia, all with varying levels of democratic participation, have caused a re-evaluation of this assumption in recent years (Fig. 2.3). Can highly autocratic political environments foster high levels of innovation? Is democracy and political freedom really an enabler of innovation?

Of course 'democracy' occurs on a spectrum and can be measured in a variety of ways and on a range of scales (local, regional, national). Some researchers make the distinction between political or

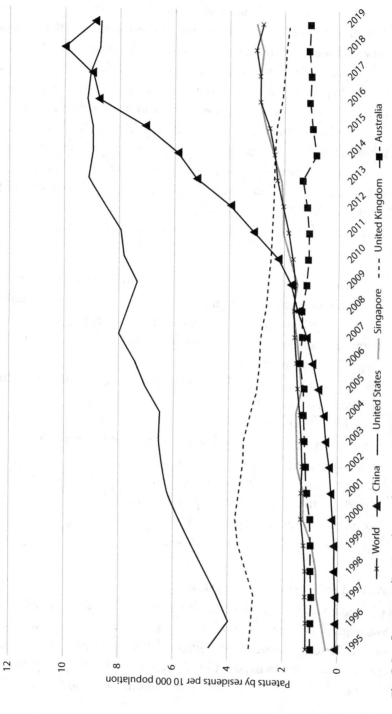

Fig. 2.3. Patent applications by residents per 10 000 population.

Patents by residents per 10 000 population

—×— World —▲— China —— United States —— Singapore - - - United Kingdom —■— Australia

parliamentary democracy and 'knowledge democracy' – that is, the freedom of information flows via institutions such as the media, academia and digital platforms (in't Veld 2010; Campbell 2019).

The impressive recent patent performance of China, however, is illustrating that the relationship is not linear, and there have been many historical examples of impressive technological development in autocratic environments (Acemoglu and Robinson 2000). It may be that China is still on the path to greater political freedom through economic advancement or, as some have suggested, that patents registered in China over recent years build on breakthrough technology developed elsewhere (Campbell 2019).

The perceived benefits of democratic environments to innovation include:

- enabling greater participation in the innovation process by cultures of inclusivity (gender, ethnicity, background, ability and sexual identity). This increases the efficiency of the human capital available for innovation by increasing the competition for high-level innovation roles
- providing long-term political stability through regular peaceful transitions of power
- providing accountability and scrutiny of public spending on innovation, thus ensuring less corruption and targeted and efficient spending
- encouraging creativity to inspire innovation through political freedom and freedom of expression, including the ability to comment on political processes
- greater ability to attract skilled people.

Innovative milieus and ecosystems

What Florida described as the 'people climate' is broadly aligned with the sociological concept of 'milieu', while the networked industrial system that Saxenian observed in Silicon Valley seemed to also relate to the ecological term 'ecosystem'. A milieu is the immediate physical and social environment (job markets, neighbourhood, housing, social circles) that crafts a person's inner narrative and their personal experience (Wright Mills 1959) and an ecosystem is the network of interdependencies between species within an environment. Both terms have experienced a resurgence when preceded with the term 'innovation' or 'startup' along with a new recognition of the importance of creating places of interaction and cultures of young entrepreneurial energy (Fig. 2.4).

The concept of the 'innovative milieu' was first introduced by the French group of researchers known as *Groupe de recherche européen sur les milieux innovateurs* (GREMI) in the 1980s. The development of an innovative milieu is enhanced by interaction spaces and collective or informal learning opportunities. These in turn boost the innovative capacity of a city or place (Maennig and Ölschläger 2011). The innovative milieu could be hothoused by mentoring, provision of collaboration opportunities, and the construction of shared spaces – often provided by local governments, chambers of commerce and industry, or supportive business networks. As the concept developed and merged with discussion of 'innovative ecosystems', a variety of informal learning spaces were encouraged to ensure that smart people

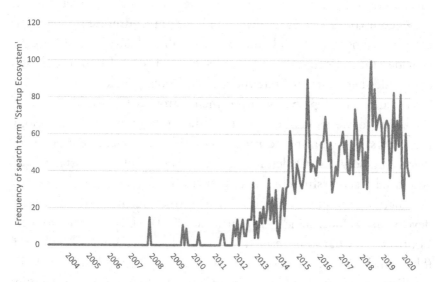

Fig. 2.4. Growth of the search term 'Startup Ecosystem' 2004–2021. Source: Google Trends.

had the opportunity to meet, discuss ideas and tinker in experimental environments. These learning spaces included coffee shops, bars, libraries, co-working spaces, maker spaces, community sheds and gardens, hackathons, pitch nights and local coding or writing competitions. The entrepreneurial or startup ecosystems were mapped and online directories created to ensure that the human capital of a region could be easily found and utilised if needed in the development of new ideas (Kruger and Caccopi 2014; Startup Muster 2017; StartupAUS 2020; European Commission 2021).

The digital age and the focus on entrepreneurialism

The publication of Saxenian and Florida's books also coincided with a new focus on regional entrepreneurialism in the emerging online and digital age from the 1990s onwards. The ability of lean digital companies to scale up to powerful global enterprises within just a few years led to a new generation of tech developers who pursued a 'winner takes all' strategy in the race for network dominance. Google, Amazon, PayPal and Facebook were the leaders in a cohort of digital companies that were assisted by greater broadband connectivity and the introduction of mobile and smart phones. The sudden emergence of these companies placed a new emphasis on coding skills and the creation of new online platforms across all industries. The need to provide cultural support for those seeds of ideas and budding digital companies began to infiltrate the minds of policy makers.

By around 2005, many governments around the world had been awakened to the economic benefit of funding or supporting technology incubators, co-working centres and, in particular, entrepreneur mentoring services (Özdemir and Şehitoğlu 2013). Some states even employed a successful 'chief entrepreneur' to attract talent from other jurisdictions and bring them into their startup precincts to inspire local developers (Queensland Government 2021). Digital technologies flourished in what some termed the 'technological Cambrian explosion' (Shrinath V 2017). Global platforms, the Internet of Things, artificial intelligence, virtual and augmented reality, blockchain and robotics began to disrupt large and established business models in all sectors.

Creating entrepreneurs who could see new applications for the emerging digital technology in order to disrupt and create disproportionate wealth meant carefully cultivating the creative, innovative and entrepreneurial spirits in supportive communities, milieus and ecosystems.

Supporting and keeping the people within the innovation ecosystem also meant supporting lifestyle and cultural institutions. Museums, art galleries, theatres, live music venues, active transport, microbreweries and craft beers, parks and recreational facilities were all added to the lists of potentially magnetic features expected of a location attempting to attract digital talent. As the global competition for the digitally skilled increased, so did selling the regional cultural and lifestyle attributes (Florida 2006).

The problems with culture-led innovation efforts: displacement, inequality and opportunity loss

In many countries, the huge success of Saxenian's and Florida's books turned policy makers' attention to their cultural and industrial mix and inspired many urban revitalisation projects in downtown precincts. Cities around the world tried to attract young, tech-savvy creatives and foster startups and entrepreneurialism as a means of fostering economic development.

The sudden spending on public arts, parks, co-working centres, community gardens, farmers' markets, coffee strips, maker spaces and cultural centres saw accelerated gentrification in previously rundown city centres, and the broad displacement of income-poor creatives to new rundown suburbs on the fringes of the city. Meanwhile, property developers capitalised on inner-city density regulations to quickly erect, large, cheaply constructed towers of apartments that were often targeted at the investment, rather than residential, market.

Some of these revitalised areas lacked the social infrastructure of schools, health facilities and green spaces to make them attractive to working- or middle-class demographics. The rise of the sharing economy – in particular accommodation companies such as Airbnb – also resulted in buyer-investors leaving large sections of popular lifestyle centres vacant and unavailable to permanent tenants, with many longer-term residents suddenly struggling to pay skyrocketing rents. The very factors that made the downtown, inner-city areas attractive to creative project workers – cheap rent, large warehouse spaces, and in some cases the availability of *ad hoc* music venues – were suddenly eliminated in the gentrification process that only served to fragment creative communities and exile them to the outer suburbs or rural areas.

Florida's recipe for economic success quickly attracted criticism from the residents of the gentrifying locations. It also gained critics in urban planning who had started examining the impacts of the inner-city revival movement on inequality, homelessness and the resulting geographic segregation between service workers and the newly developing urban elite. Many of Florida's critics evoked Jane Jacobs, the Canadian–American urban activist who rallied against urban renewal projects in the 1960s.

Florida's later book, *The New Urban Crisis: How our cities are increasing inequality, deepening segregation, and failing the middle class – and what we can do about it* (Florida 2018) tries to address much of this criticism. Florida suggests that mayors of cities are the new captains of economic development and that more powers of government should be devolved to the local level to allow them to adequately deal with emerging issues of inequality and class segregation. Despite these recommendations, many of the policies to address growing inequality (such as taxation policies, welfare and education funding) are still, and are likely to remain, functions of higher levels of government, while the middle-class jobs are still often found in the large organisations Florida suggested were no longer attractive to creative workers.

Although downtown urban renewal projects are seen to be hip and attractive to creative people, undertaking an urban renewal project is no guarantee that creative people will move in. Changing the culture and attitudes of existing communities is also difficult. Someone who is homophobic, xenophobic and untrained in technological skills is unlikely to take up a coding course and suddenly become more tolerant (meeting Florida's technology, talent and tolerance criteria, for instance). The only way many of those cultures are going to change is through population displacement, or a new demographic moving in. The mix of cultural and social attitudes may then create conflict between the two groups: the resistant early residents and the more open-minded newcomers.

Liveability and the cultural attractiveness of a locale may also not equate with increased innovation or technology development. Cities such as Vienna in Austria, Melbourne and Sydney in Australia, and Osaka in Japan are in the top five of *The Economist*'s most liveable cities but are not in the top 10 of the OECD's most innovative cities (Table 2.1). This may, of course, be a result of differences in the measurements for the indices for liveability compared to those assessed by Florida – which included a 'Bohemian' and a Gay index – or a lag in the effects of liveability on innovation. It is wrong to put too much emphasis on the two very different indices, but it does broadly demonstrate that liveability alone does not equal innovation outcomes.

Spending on urban renewal to attract young, tech-savvy creatives or to create a startup ecosystem may not necessarily build innovation or create new industries.

Much like place-led innovation approaches, culture-led innovation has seen a wave of policy enthusiasts followed by a wave of critics, but

Table 2.1. Liveability compared to innovativeness

The Economist's Liveability Ranks 2021[a]	Innovation Cities™ Index 2021[b]
1. Auckland, New Zealand	1. Tokyo, Japan
2. Osaka, Japan	2. Boston, US
3. Adelaide, Australia	3. New York, US
4. Wellington, New Zealand	4. Sydney, Australia
5. Tokyo, Japan	5. Singapore, Singapore
6. Perth, Australia	6. Dallas–Fort Worth, US
7. Zurich, Switzerland	7. Seoul, South Korea
7. Geneva, Switzerland	8. Houston, US
9. Melbourne, Australia	9. Chicago, US
10. Brisbane, Australia	10. Paris, France

[a] The Economist Intelligence Unit (2021).
[b] Innovation Cities Program (2021). Source: 2thinknow Innovation Cities™ Index 2021: www.innovation-cities.com/indexes/

actions to support culture-led innovation are part of the overall picture for policy makers to consider when trying to find the right mix for enhancing innovation and creating new industries in a particular location.

Table 2.2. Advantages and disadvantages of culture-led innovation efforts

Advantages	Disadvantages
• Improving liveability and cultural institutions lies within the purview of local and state governments, so funds for spending are usually available at a local level. • Urban renewal projects can sometimes be 'mixed use' development, combining business, residential and education facilities. This means funds for public development can sometimes be leveraged from the private sector, and affordable housing for students and low-income demographics can be incorporated if planned well. • Creating networks of entrepreneurs and talented technologists can take advantage of the ability of new digital technologies to scale rapidly and provide strong employment growth. • Urban renewal and culture-based approaches can bring together many parties with an interest in land use, such as education institutions, business groups and chambers of commerce and government agencies.	• Changing culture is difficult on a city or regional level and takes time. It is no easy task to change attitudes or culture or suddenly build tight networks of supportive, innovative and risk-taking entrepreneurs. It takes time and often ongoing or sustained funding. • Urban renewal or revitalisation projects can displace large demographics through causing skyrocketing rents. Incoming populations of creatives may also displace residents, creating conflict between the new and old populations. Or if the area has built a reputation for being creative, that creative community may need to move to access cheaper spaces. • There may not be land available for large urban renewal projects, or the renewal projects require too much land for building acquisition to be successful. • Over-development by property developers seeking to sell cheap apartments to investors in revitalised areas may neglect the educational facilities, green space and transport infrastructure required to service city-based populations. • Spending on liveability or cultural institutions may not necessarily result in high levels of innovativeness or entrepreneurialism.

Successful culture-led innovation: The Docklands, Melbourne

In the 1990s, the former and largely derelict cargo docks and adjacent industrial land just south of the Melbourne CBD became the centre of one of Australia's largest urban renewal projects: Docklands.

The Docklands area was once Victoria's primary port but had fallen out of use in the 1950s and 1960s when container cargo began to be shipped to modern off-loading facilities further down the river at the new Port of Melbourne. Derelict and disused, the warehouses and large industrial spaces close to the Melbourne's city centre started to gain a reputation for artistic, counterculture living with the warehouses being perfect atmospheric venues for large 'rave', 'house' and New Years' Eve dance parties from the 1980s onwards.

In 1991, the Docklands Authority, later VicUrban, was formed to oversee the redevelopment of over 200 ha of docks and urban land. Several urban developers and master planners were engaged to develop a mixed-use precinct that included residential areas, hotels, a business and technology park, a film and television complex, entertainment venues, a sports stadium, marinas and waterfront and commercial space. The redevelopment area is so large that it was divided into eight precincts, each being constructed by a different commercial developer. Public art and green space were made central features of all precincts.

After a series of plans that did not come to fruition, a new sports stadium was finally opened in March 2000 and this accelerated development of nearby residential areas and commercial space (Fig. 2.5).

The Docklands development now houses over 13 000 residents and the national headquarters of two of Australia's four major banks, as well as media corporations, Australia's Bureau of Meteorology, global technology organisations, startup incubators and large retail organisations. It has attracted over $14.6 billion in private investment, accommodates more than 73 000 workers and showcases 68 major pieces of public art. New studio facilities at Docklands are boosting the development of screen industries in the state – film, television, augmented and virtual reality applications and video games. Startup fintech companies from Docklands incubators are also working with the resident banks to develop blockchain, mobile and cybersecurity solutions for Australia and export. The development has the largest concentration of green buildings in Australia and, with over 9 ha of parks and open space, it is

Fig. 2.5. Melbourne Docklands Development 2007 by Joe.Bekker is licenced under CC BY-SA 3.0.

embracing ecologically sustainable development principles (Development Victoria 2021).

While the redevelopment has also attracted criticism for failing to accommodate families by not including schools or pedestrian access to Melbourne's CBD, these are now being built.

In 2019 Melbourne was ranked 11th in the world (first in Australia) by the Innovation Cities Program, although this dropped to 33rd post-pandemic in 2021 (Innovation Cities Program 2019, 2021).

Where culture-led innovation effort has been less successful: San Antonio, Texas

San Antonio, in south-west Texas, is a bicultural, bilingual mix of Mexican and American society. It is the seventh largest city in the US, with nearly 1.5 million residents, and is now the fastest growing city in America (Ura and Daniel 2018).

The rapid growth in San Antonio has not been without problems and the city suffers from geographic racial segregation and high rates of poverty. Unemployment in San Antonio is lower than the US average at just 2.9% (November 2019); however, income levels are also 14% less than the US average.

In 2011, the City of San Antonio government set out to transform its sleepy and partially vacant downtown area into a vibrant city centre through a visionary *SA 2020* economic development plan. A $10 million investment in downtown improvements in 2007 rapidly grew to over $170 million in 2017, as the city invested in public art, river walks and parks revitalisation, tax incentives for residential housing developments, public building refurbishments, and the transformation of previous industrial buildings – such as breweries and fair sites – into parks, hotels and apartments (Fig. 2.6). This public spending leveraged significant private and federal government investment, including an expansion of the downtown campus of the University of Texas. This included a $33 million National Security Collaboration Center and a $57 million School of Data Science, both of which work with two nearby military bases. Since 2011, the downtown area has seen 64 new building developments that have added 6810 housing units and significant new office and retail space.

By the end of 2018, however, complaints about the city's gentrification and a lack of opportunity for existing residents started to feed back to elected officials. The Mayor's Housing Policy Task Force found that median house prices had doubled since 2005 while incomes had risen only 40%. Housing affordability was beginning to be a challenge for many long-term residents as half the city's renters were spending more than a third of their income on rent. Many families that could no longer afford the downtown areas moved to the outer suburbs, and San Antonio has also seen significant suburban sprawl that has placed pressure on the roads and transport systems.

Despite the potential of San Antonio to attract further business and property investment in its urban transformation, the potential for building innovative new industries and a thriving technology centre seems less clear, while the challenges associated with increased inequality and housing affordability are very real:

> *The vision of San Antonio being peddled by developers – that of an emerging tech center anchoring a blossoming downtown – runs into hard truths when considered with the entire city in mind. Building a truly equitable tech district for the whole community means providing pathways for local talent.*
>
> *'Many people want to expand the high-tech corridor in San Antonio, but it's a balancing act,' says Caine. 'The city has historically low levels of education, making it difficult for tech firms to relocate here.' Ian Caine, Director of the Center for Urban and Regional Planning Research at the University of Texas at San Antonio quoted in (Sisson 2018).*

Only 26% of San Antonio residents have a bachelor's degree. Thirty-three per cent of those bachelor's degrees, however, have been gained in the sciences, including 5% in computing, mathematics and statistics and 6% in engineering. The city does not yet feature on highly on any rankings of global

Fig. 2.6.   San Antonio River Walk by Zereshk is licenced under CC BY-SA 3.0.

innovative cities. Innovation Cities Program 2021 ranks San Antonio 48th in global rankings and 23rd in the US although, impressively, it has jumped 22 places up the global rankings since 2019 (Innovation Cities Program 2021).

It may be too early to see the real outcomes of culture-led innovation in San Antonio but the experience of San Antonio exemplifies the challenges many cities face in building new industries by investing in cultural and urban renewal.

Summary

The importance of culture and industrial structure to innovation and industrial adaptability was highlighted by two bestselling books: AnnaLee Saxenian's *Regional Advantage* (1996), and Richard Florida's *The Rise of the Creative Class* (2003). These sparked numerous urban renewal projects, increased expenditure on the cultural and lifestyle assets of many regions, and led to a concentration on the highly productive networking cultures and lifestyles of younger, inner-city populations. In many cases these efforts assisted in attracting investment, but in many cases much of that investment went into property, rather than into innovative activity. That resulted in the displacement of inner-city populations and the formation of geographic wealth disparities. Lifestyle and environment alone may create economic resilience and adaptability but won't necessarily increase innovation and productivity. For this it needs to be buttressed by skills and innovation-targeted investment, which are discussed in the following chapters.

References

Acemoglu D, Robinson JA (2000) Why did the West extend the franchise? Democracy, inequality, and growth in historical perspective. *The Quarterly Journal of Economics* **115**, 1167–1199. doi:10.1162/003355300555042

Campbell DFJ (2019) *Global Quality of Democracy as Innovation Enabler: Measuring democracy for success.* Springer International Publishing, Cham, Switzerland.

Development Victoria (2021) Docklands. Melbourne. <https://www.development.vic.gov.au/projects/docklands?page=overview>

European Commission (2021) *Startup Europe: Building the ecosystem*. Brussels, <https://digital-strategy.ec.europa.eu/en/policies/startup-europe-building-ecosystem>>

Florida RL (2003) *The Rise of the Creative Class: And how it's transforming work, leisure, community and everyday life*. Pluto Press, North Melbourne, Vic.

Florida R (2005) *Flight of the Creative Class*. Harper Collins, New York.

Florida R (2018) *The New Urban Crisis: How our cities are increasing inequality, deepening segregation, and failing the middle class – and what we can do about it*. Basic Books, New York.

Innovation Cities Program (2019) *Innovation Cities^TM Index 2019: Top 100 World's most innovative cities*. 2thinknow, Melbourne.

Innovation Cities Program (2021) *Innovation Cities^TM Index 2021: Top 100 World's most innovative cities*. 2thinknow, Melbourne.

in't Veld RJit (2010) Towards knowledge democracy. In *Knowledge Democracy: Consequences for science, politics, and media*. (Ed. RJ in't Veld) pp. 1–10. Springer, Heidelberg, Germany.

Kruger M, Caccopi J (2014) Startup Ecosystem Report. Queensland Government Department of Science, Information Technology, Innovation and the Arts. Available at <https://www.qld.gov.au/dsiti/assets/documents/startup-ecosystem-mapping-report.pdf>

Maennig W, Ölschläger M (2011) Innovative milieux and regional competitiveness: the role of associations and chambers of commerce and industry in Germany. *Regional Studies* **45**, 441–452. doi:10.1080/00343401003601917

Özdemir ÖÇ, Şehitoğlu Y (2013) Assessing the impacts of technology business incubators: a framework for technology development centers in Turkey. *Procedia: Social and Behavioral Sciences* **75**, 282–291 doi:10.1016/j.sbspro.2013.04.032.

Queensland Government (2021) *Office of the Chief Entrepreneur*. Advance Queensland, Brisbane. <https://www.chiefentrepreneur.qld.gov.au/who-we-are>

Saxenian A (1996) *Regional Advantage: Culture and competition in Silicon Valley and Route 128*. Harvard University Press, Cambridge, Massachusetts.

Shrinath V (2017) The Cambrian Explosion in technology, and how it's affecting us. *The Economic Times, India*. 18 February

Sisson P (2018) San Antonio, the nation's fastest-growing city, sees downtown rebound. A 300-year-old capital of Latinx culture on the cusp of change. *Curbed*, New York, 23 October. <https://archive.curbed.com/2018/10/23/18011174/san-antonio-river-walk-real-estate-development>

StartupAUS (2020) Crossroads: An action plan to develop a world leading tech startup ecosystem in Australia. StartupAUS, Sydney.

Startup Muster (2017) *Startup Muster 2017 Annual Report.* <https://www.startupmuster.com/reports/Startup-Muster-2017-Report.pdf>

The Economist Intelligence Unit (2021) The Global Liveability Index 2021: How the COVID 19 pandemic affected liveability worldwide. *The Economist*, London. <https://www.eiu.com/n/campaigns/global-liveability-index-2021/>

Ura A, Daniel A (2018) San Antonio tops national list in population gain. *The Texas Tribune*, Austin, 24 May

Wright Mills C (1959) *The Sociological Imagination.* Oxford University Press, Oxford.

3

Skills-led innovation

Aim

To increase innovation outcomes through attracting or training skilled people

'Knowledge is power. Information is liberating. Education is the premise of progress, in every society, in every family.' In 1997, United Nations Secretary-General Kofi Annan extended Sir Francis Bacon's famous aphorism 'ipsa scientia potestas est' or 'knowledge is power' to outline the central role of knowledge and education in economic and societal progress (Annan 1997). Education, or the development of knowledge and skills through education, is a central input in innovation indicators (Fig. 3.1). Without capable, knowledgeable people, there is no progress through innovation.

Innovation and new industry development require people with creativity and good ideas, as well as the same or different people with the skills to develop or adopt those ideas to create new products, services, processes, firms and industries – that is, to innovate.

People are generally not born with the skills required to innovate: they need to be taught them through formal education (schools, technical institutions and universities), industrial experience (on-the-job training or firm-based learning) or a conducive and motivating learning environment (through access to knowledge and experimental forums via family, friends, hobby groups, or online or self-directed learning) (Fig. 3.2).

In terms of regional economics, skills can be developed in the population through training and education, through spillovers of

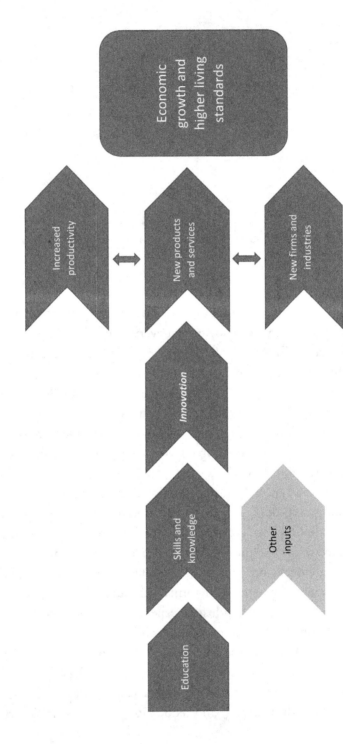

Fig. 3.1. Education and skills acquisition: the fuel for innovation.

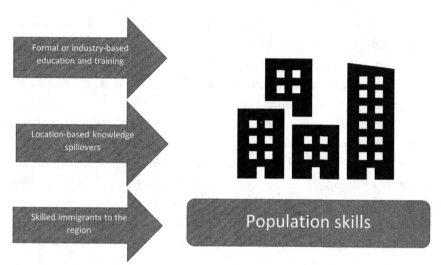

Fig. 3.2. Sources of population skills.

knowledge between people and firms, or through attracting skilled people from elsewhere.

The main focus for many governments seeking to stimulate innovation through skills development has been support for formal training avenues and ensuring that training is linked to industry or industry needs. The OECD states:

> OECD countries have long emphasised the development of
> skilled people through education and training, in recognition
> of the positive link between human capital and economic
> growth and productivity (OECD 2011).

Investing in education and skills for economic development is a subset of human capital theory. This broadly states that investing in people through providing health, education, transport and housing services pays off in economic growth (World Bank 2020). Education is by far the most studied element of human capital theory, and human capital theory is sometimes referred to as 'the economics of education' (Quiggin 1999; Fitzsimons 2017). Because education benefits individuals, organisations and society, there is constant tension regarding who should pay for education and training – the individual, the business sector or the taxpayer.

The links between formal education and training and greater rates of innovation are not entirely clear, however. While there is huge investment and general agreement that improving national innovation rates requires skills enhancement, it is difficult to know what skills to invest in for innovation outcomes – especially as the skills that a society needs for its industries to remain profitable and regionally or globally competitive are constantly changing.

In 2011, the OECD conducted a comprehensive review of the literature to help OECD policy makers better understand what skills a country should invest in. Their publication *Skills for Innovation and Research* cites evidence confirming the broad link between the national investment in skills and innovation outcomes. This evidence includes:

- a US study that found 'The presence of an educated workforce is the decisive factor that explains the inventive output of cities, even after controlling for the historical mix of industries and technologies invented' (Carlino *et al.* 2009; Carlino and Hunt 2009)
- a Spanish study that found human capital to be positively related to patent applications: 'A region's own R&D activities and human capital are observed to have a positive significant effect on innovation output, measured by the number of patents' (Gumbau-Albert and Maudos 2009)
- another US study that found that workers engaged in 'new work' – innovative roles resulting from technological adoption or adaptation – are more likely to be in regions with high educational attainment: 'All else equal, workers are more likely to be observed in new work in locations initially dense in college graduates and industry variety' (Lin 2011).

In addition to the OECD-cited studies, more recent work by Diebolt and Hippe used large longitudinal datasets that recorded innovation and entrepreneurships in Europe over the last 150 years. Diebolt and Hippe found that 'human capital is the most significant historical factor related to current patent applications per capita and current GDP per capita' (Diebolt and Hippe 2019).

The link between skills and innovation is hard to establish because of the vague and inconsistent definitions and measures of 'innovation' and 'skills'.

Patent activity is a commonly cited proxy for innovation due to the fact that it is well measured, there are often centuries of data available and it can be linked to location (or at least the location as written on the patent application, which is often the company headquarters rather than the location in which the patented idea was first thought of or developed). It is far from perfect as an innovation measure because it is more likely to pick up product innovation, which is more likely to be patented, than process innovation. A large number of patents also do not go on to create innovation; they are never developed or commercialised into products or create any economic impact. Some studies prefer to focus on the impacts of education on research and development (R&D) or productivity (particularly firm, total factor or multifactor productivity) instead of innovation as measured by patents (Ramos *et al.* 2010).

Educational attainment is also a commonly used proxy for skills or human capital (Hofheinz 2009; Rabiul Islam *et al.* 2014), although this is by far not the only measure, and it also implies that educational attainment is linear, rather than multidirectional over a lifetime (McGuirk *et al.* 2015; Marginson 2019).

Despite these difficulties, it does appear that rates of innovation and the creation of new products and industries may occur at greater rates around education institutions that teach people how to create new knowledge. This is especially true for higher education institutions, such as universities and technical colleges. Valero and Van Reenen examined large UNESCO datasets for nearly 1500 regions across 78 countries and found:

> Our estimates imply that doubling the number of universities per capita is associated with 4% higher future GDP per capita. Furthermore, there appear to be positive spillover effects from universities to geographically close neighbouring regions. ... Part of the effect of universities on growth is

mediated through an increased supply of human capital and greater innovation (although the magnitudes are not large) (Valero and Van Reenen 2016).

Places of learning not only transfer knowledge and skills to a new generation, but also they attract knowledgeable and skilled people from other parts of the world. This is through providing employment, providing interesting and fulfilling research work, being able to attract R&D funding, and forming partnerships with industry in experimenting with new product and process development. In this way they can also contribute to the development of local skills through inward migration and knowledge spillovers.

Despite what seems to be a well-supported case for investment in human capital or skills through education, the 2011 OECD report also notes:

> Overall there appeared to be very little correlation between measures of skill and innovation ... Innovation outputs are a result of a complex web of inputs and other interactions with the broader economic environment ... Innovation is a multifaceted and complex undertaking and simply adding inputs may not achieve the desired outcomes (OECD 2011, p. 78).

Inputs associated with skills or human capital sit alongside other innovation inputs such as R&D spending, technological adoption and infrastructure. The lack of clarity on the link between skills and innovation may also be due, in part, to the broad range of skills that may be acquired, and that some skills may have greater impacts on innovation than others. Determining what skills to invest in for the best innovation outcomes, or what mix of skills creates the best innovation outcomes is, again, difficult. It may be that what is most needed in rapidly changing economic environments is merely structured education or business experience that teaches people to learn and gives them the confidence to be adaptable and opportunistic.

Hard or soft skills? STEM or the humanities?

By far the most heated debate on skills-based innovation has been whether policy makers and education institutions should invest in skills in the fields of science, technology, engineering and mathematics (STEM) or the humanities (arts, history, philosophy, languages and literature). This has been compounded by apparent skills shortages in technical and scientific fields in many areas of new product development and innovation, and calls for a greater focus on STEM education. The US Department of Defense, for instance, says 'Diminishing USA STEM education and industrial jobs, both … have a deleterious effect on the industrial base's ability to sustain itself and to innovate' and regards diminishing STEM skills in the US as a 'macro-force' leading to national deficiencies in both manufacturing and defence capabilities (US Department of Defense 2020).

There is some evidence that STEM skills promote higher levels of innovation, particularly for product innovation resulting in new patents. It is these new patented products that then go on to spawn new industries. New firm creation has been found to be greater around universities that specialise in basic sciences, applied sciences and engineering, but not around universities that specialise in humanities and social sciences (Bonaccorsi *et al*. 2013). Certain STEM skills – such as spatial ability – have been associated with higher rates of innovation and the generation of new products (as measured by patents and publications). This may be due to the unique role of spatial abilities in verbal and mathematical reasoning (Harrison *et al*. 2013; Taylor and Hutton 2013). At a company level, the capacity to innovate has been positively associated with the availability of scientists and engineers (Santa *et al*. 2019).

The impact of skills on regional innovation is also affected by the industrial specialities, industry structure and the level of technological advancement of enterprises in that region (OECD 2011). For instance, the skills that have the greatest impact on innovation in the creative area of Hollywood, California, are different from the skills that would impact innovation in the growing tech hub of Austin, Texas, or the skills that would benefit the small rural coffee-producing regions of Vietnam. The skills required for product innovation (often engineering and design skills) differ from the skills required for process innovation (often managerial, strategic, team-building and financial skills). The OECD suggests that the skill set required to boost innovation may depend on the type of innovation desired and the existing industry structure (OECD 2011). The impact of skills may also be a function of a region's 'distance from the technological frontier' – or relative state of technological advancement (Vandenbussche *et al.* 2006).

Highly technologically advanced regions that are already using technology to its maximum benefit have more to gain from STEM skills that can create new products; that is, they need to push the technological frontier forward. Less technologically advanced regions have more to gain from softer, people-oriented skills that can improve firm productivity through process innovation and technology adoption. Put simply, the skills needed to adopt existing technologies are different from the skills needed to create new technologies and products (Fig. 3.3). Although they didn't break it down by hard or soft skills, Vandenbussche *et al.* (2006) found that 'skilled human capital has a stronger growth-enhancing effect in economies which are closer to the technological frontier'. STEM skills involved in new product innovation may be more important to technologically advanced regions.

Over the last few decades, there has been a relative decline in several OECD countries in the proportion of graduates in the science and engineering disciplines compared to graduates in social sciences, business

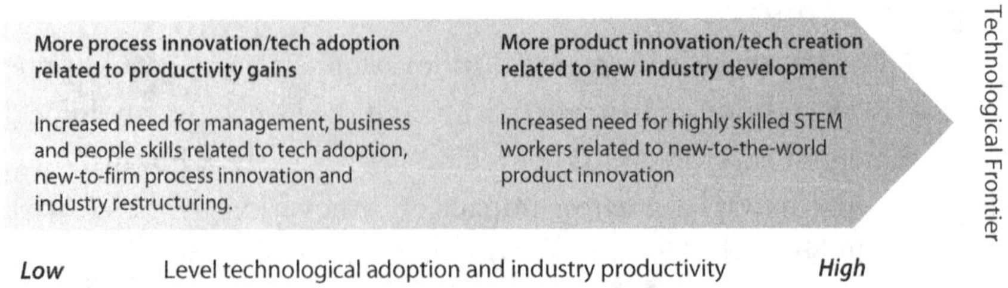

More process innovation/tech adoption related to productivity gains	More product innovation/tech creation related to new industry development	Technological Frontier
Increased need for management, business and people skills related to tech adoption, new-to-firm process innovation and industry restructuring.	Increased need for highly skilled STEM workers related to new-to-the-world product innovation	

Low   Level technological adoption and industry productivity   *High*

Fig. 3.3. Skills needed to innovate depend on the region's distance from the technology frontier.

and law. The services sector, interestingly, employs more science and technology graduates in OECD countries than the manufacturing sector. In the manufacturing sector, however, R&D personnel were positively correlated with subsequent in-house product innovation (OECD 2011).

As education institutions in some countries started to cut back on humanities programs in the wake of a new emphasis on STEM skills in the early 2000s, people working in the humanities areas began to mount a defence of the role of their fields by highlighting the critical role interpersonal and other non-STEM skills will have in the future workforce. The World Economic Forum, for instance, predicts that 'top' skills required for employment 2025 will be a mix of social and emotional skills (often gained through studying the humanities) as well as technical skills. These include:

1. Analytical thinking and innovation
2. Active learning and learning strategies
3. Complex problem-solving
4. Critical thinking and analysis
5. Creativity, originality and initiative (World Economic Forum 2020).

Workers with these skills may utilise STEM workers and their technical knowledge but would typically come from humanities and business backgrounds.

Even firms that invest heavily in R&D and build new technologies and products need people with non-STEM skills if they are to be successful. For instance, blockchain is one of the new fourth industrial revolution technologies. Many people don't understand it as a technology or understand how it could potentially help a business or organisation, although there is widespread experimentation with it across different industries. In 2020, LinkedIn stated that blockchain skills were the skills most highly sought-after by recruiters using the platform. A closer look at what skills employers were seeking specifically in regards to potential candidates found that they sought a mix of 'soft' and 'hard' skills. The 'hard' skills included software engineering and coding skills, and the 'soft' skills included creativity, communication and leadership. Atherton *et al.* (2020) suggested 'for blockchain to enter a mass adoption phase, the industry will need employees with an integrated skills set of both hard software engineering skills and soft behavioural or enterprise skills'.

The OECD also suggests that the importance of 'soft skills', including communication and teamwork, may gain importance as the economy continues to globalise and technologies such as artificial intelligence (AI), robotics and cloud-based services replace increasing numbers of routinised jobs in technical professions (OECD 2011). Technology commentators also suggest that the human-based attributes will be the ones sought after as the new wave of digital technologies are more widely adopted; attributes that involve empathy, creativity, strategic thinking, questioning and dreaming (Marr 2018).

Unlocking the potential of skilled people at work

Cultures within organisations play a significant role in determining the innovative capacity of a region though their utilisation of human capital. Work done by Australia's National Vocational Education and Training Research and Evaluation Program found that firms' 'innovative capacity' was related to the management of people, the development of a learning culture at work and a firm's external links to education institutions (Smith *et al.* 2012). Practices such as building small, high-performance teams, creating more team-based work, providing workplace training and flexible work options all resulted in higher firm innovation rates. McGuirk *et al.* (2015) also found that firms, especially small firms, that employed 'innovative human capital' or people with high levels of education and training as well as attributes such as 'willingness to change' and 'high job satisfaction', were indeed more likely to innovate.

Inspiring or playful office environments with interaction spaces such as communal kitchens, barbecues, coffee machines, lounge areas, indoor games areas or creative walls can also instil a sense of creative freedom. Greater workplace interactions increase the sharing and cross-pollination of ideas impacting on organisational innovation, although their effects are not clear. Steve Jobs, co-founder of Apple Computers and then Pixar Animation Studios, used centralised communal areas and interaction points – such as the cafeteria, mailboxes and meetings – to increase incidental talk and organisational innovation, while Google is famous for its playroom-type offices, which have included bean bags, hammocks, free lunches and inter-floor slippery slides (Dunne 2014).

Skills through knowledge spillovers

Learning environments can extend beyond the organisation to the social and cultural environment of a region or place. As described in Chapters 1 and 2, knowledge spillovers resulting from co-located firms operating in the same industry can encourage learning and skills development through a kind of environmental and cultural immersion.

Innovation and R&D centres in most countries are highly spatially concentrated, even within large industrial zones. The spillovers that innovative firms benefit from by being so tightly co-located include sharing suppliers and workers and transferring knowledge. These benefits decrease sharply within short distances, with the majority of gains being experienced when firms are located within just 1.6 km of each other (Carlino and Kerr 2015; Buzard *et al.* 2020). Innovative clusters and creative environments can inspire learning and skills development and, in some cases, reduce the need for formal learning.

Famously, Apple and Microsoft founders Steve Jobs and Bill Gates gave up on their formal studies to start their now global businesses after learning basic computer skills in their high schools and local computer clubs. As discussed in Chapter 2, Professor Fred Terman, Dean of the School of Engineering at Stanford University, encouraged his students to start businesses based on their research and patented technologies rather than undertake further academic study and postgraduate education. That the immediate environment could support people to learn and develop these skills, create new businesses and gain substantial investment was due to the tightly networked learning and investment environment around them (Saxenian 1996).

The benefits of migration: attracting skilled people and encouraging them to stay

'Key people bring in other key people' was advice given to me by Paul Lucas, who was Minister for Innovation and the Information Economy (2001–2004) and one of the key ministers responsible for the 'Smart State' agenda in Queensland, Australia. 'If you focus on attracting and appointing the right people, clusters will build themselves.'

In nearly all innovation hotspots, there are key people who have had a vision to create a new products or business models and the political or financial influence to initiate growth in emerging industries. While many of these key people are deeply embedded in their fields of expertise and understand the science and capabilities of the emerging work, the qualities that have enabled them to build new companies and industries include political persuasiveness, optimism, foresight, communication and media skills, and a charisma that made them a magnet for other highly skilled and innovative individuals. Fred Terman, William Shockley, Steve Jobs, Elon Musk, Bill Gates and Jeff Bezos are examples of people in and around Silicon Valley who have had to influence and inspire large organisations, shareholders, venture capitalists and politicians in order to attract funding for their innovations and now global enterprises.

The migration flows of graduates and whether or not locally trained graduates can stay in a region through employment opportunities both affect how effective higher education institutions are in local innovation outcomes.

Faggian and McCann (2009) found that inter-regional flows of university graduates in the UK had more impact on economic growth than the internal generation of new graduates from local universities. This suggests graduates immediately move to areas with attractive work opportunities and lifestyles or to areas where they can create new businesses. Graduates have seeds of ideas that need fertile soil and a nurturing environment in which to grow. The 'hothouse' metaphor has become common in narratives of nurturing innovation (Finnestrand *et al.* 2015; The Economist 2017; Simonsson 2021).

Faggian and McCann's findings also challenged the cluster economics put forward by Michael E Porter because they suggested small firms and population densities were negatively associated with innovation:

> [W]e find no evidence of any role played by small firms in regional innovation. Our results are in stark contrast to the 'learning regions' and 'knowledge regions' literature in which small firms are a central tenet of the hypothesised innovation mechanisms. ... population density is always negatively related to innovation performance. ... As such, our findings provide a fundamental twist on the previous arguments regarding regional high technology innovation (Faggian and McCann 2009).

Since young skilled labour is so mobile, the other innovation inputs are seen as critical in turning the human capital into innovation outcomes. These include R&D spending, government contracts or collaborations, venture capital, and training in commercialisation and entrepreneurialism. The lifestyles offered by a region are also important, although this might depend on the target demographic of skills needed. Pugh O'Mara suggested that the availability of land in locations desirable to middle class professionals is critical to creating a new Silicon Valley, while Florida suggests that funky inner-city urban environments are what the young up-and-coming technologists want, and that suburban technology parks are no longer attractive (Florida 2003; Pugh O'Mara 2005).

The attraction and utilisation of global talent through migration is a central theme of Harvard Business School professor William Kerr. In his book *Gift of Global Talent: How migration shapes business, economy & society* (2019), Kerr states:

> This talent moves around a lot. The teams at Apple or Siemens or the London School of Economics draw people from far and wide, accomplishing more together than they ever could in isolation. Much of the innovative power

unleashed during the twentieth century came from global talent flowing to where it could be most productive and to where it had the capacity to realise its potential to change the world (Kerr 2019a).

Kerr (2019a,b) makes three main points about global talent in 2018:

1. talent has become the world's most precious resource – more valuable than land, infrastructure and other labour
2. talent has become increasingly mobile and there is now intense global competition for it
3. talent is shaped by the environment it finds itself in.

To attract global talent and skills, many countries have developed skilled and high-skilled migration schemes, and these schemes have become more competitive in recent years (Brucker 2015; National Academies of Science Engineering and Medicine 2015).

Skilled immigrants, or even unskilled immigrants, create multiple positive impacts on innovation levels. In many countries, immigrants are more likely to start new businesses than their native-born counterparts and they are over-represented in the STEM workforce. Foreign-born workers in the US, for instance, are more likely than native-born workers to obtain a patent, and they account for an increasing proportion of US patents in the fields of computing, electronics, medical devices and pharmaceuticals (American Immigration Council 2017). A 2003 National Survey of College Graduates (US) found that immigrants patent at double the rate of native-born Americans due to disproportionately holding science and engineering qualifications. A 1 per cent increase in immigrant college graduates increases patents per capita by 9–18 per cent (Hunt and Gauthier-Loiselle 2010).

A quarter of all high-tech companies founded in the US between 1995 and 2005 had at least one foreign-born founder, and over 40 per cent of Fortune 500 companies were founded by an immigrant or child of an immigrant (American Immigration Council 2017). This includes companies such as Google, Apple and Tesla. In 2015, close to

20 per cent of the US STEM workforce were foreign born, compared to 17 per cent in the general workforce (US Bureau of Labor Statistics 2020). In Australia, 30 per cent of the population are foreign born, but 36 per cent of startup founders in 2018 were foreign born (Startup Muster 2018).

There is no doubt that the attraction of skilled workers from other parts of the world can significantly boost local innovation levels, and skilled and inventive workplaces, such as universities and R&D institutions, can be magnets for those workers.

The problems with skills-led innovation efforts: misaligned with industry needs, unsatisfying for students, and a lack of local opportunity

As outlined above, skilled people need to be matched with opportunities for them to utilise their skills and education. As the OECD (2011) suggests, increasing the amount of education and training available may not improve regional innovation if there are few opportunities for graduates within the region, or if they can easily move to places where they can work for higher rewards. Under these conditions, skilled people will leave.

Similarly, if industry within a region cannot find the skilled and trained people it needs to innovate or even operate, it will need to undertake the costs of importing skilled people, outsource tasks to companies located elsewhere, or operate below its desired productivity and production level, and thus run the risk of becoming less profitable and competitive. During the COVID-19 pandemic in 2020, one in five businesses in Australia reported they could not find the skilled workers needed for their business operations. This included many businesses seeking STEM professionals (Australian Bureau of Statistics 2020).

Aligning the training and education provided by local institutions to the needs of the local labour market is likely to improve both graduate retention and the innovativeness of regional enterprises.

Work by Florida and Gaetani (2018) has also found that while city areas in the US with higher concentrations of universities are more innovative, they are also more economically and geographically segregated. Better integrating local education and university-led R&D efforts to local industry may help reduce the negative impacts of world-leading higher education institutions.

Likewise, education and training needs to be matched to the interests and ambitions of students undertaking the course. Around 25 per cent of Australian undergraduate university students between 2005 and 2015 left their studies before completing their degree. Around 20 per cent of students during that time stated they considered leaving their course because their expectations had not been met, their course was boring or they lacked interest in it (Universities Australia 2020). Education is more than vocational training and, in a rapidly changing world, having the skills to adapt and consider new pathways for both economic and emotional survival is increasingly important. Creating interesting courses with pathways to fulfilling careers may also assist in creating more efficient outcomes from education spending.

The success behind locations such as Silicon Valley lies not just in the availability of skilled graduates in emerging fields – such as electrical engineering and computer programming – but in attracting talent from around the world and having work contracts, venture capital and R&D jobs readily available nearby. It is important for education institutions to align their skills to opportunities available in local industries and for jobs in these industries to have globally competitive wages and lifestyles. Without transition pathways to local opportunities that can utilise the skills learnt in education institutions, skilled people will leave. The flight of local skills will then become limiting to the innovation potential of the region more generally.

As the OECD (2011) also put it:

> More broadly, given the wide variety of influences on innovation, getting policy right on skills is necessary but not sufficient to support innovative activity. Policy must be coherent and provide a supportive overall environment for innovation in which people can use their skills to their best ability.

Table 3.1. Advantages and disadvantages of skills-led innovation efforts

Advantages	Disadvantages
• Skilled and creative people are necessary for innovation, and can be gained through: - formal training - knowledge and training spillovers found in local industry clusters - migration of skilled people. • STEM and hard skills have been associated with higher rates of product innovation – essential to new industry development and job creation. • 'Softer' skills involving communication, critical and strategic thinking, creativity and collaboration are also important in applying process innovation, and in conveying and navigating the societal impacts of innovation and technological change. Process innovation is important for improvements in local firm productivity. • Investing in education and skilled people will increase the ability of the region to attract more skilled people.	• Education and training provided may not meet the needs of local industry. • Universities can contribute to economic and spatial inequality due to their highly skilled workforce and their ability to attract high-technology firms into their proximity. • Education alone is not enough to improve innovation, it needs to be combined with other innovation inputs to achieve good outcomes.

Successful skills-led innovation efforts in the New York Tech Sector

When the Global Financial Crisis (GFC) hit in 2008, New York was at its epicentre. Employment in the hardest hit sector, the financial sector centred in Wall Street, was responsible for almost 30 per cent of private sector wages in the New York City as well as 20 per cent of tax revenue for the state as a whole (New York State Labor Department 2020). Over the next 2 years, unemployment in New York City would rise from 4.4 per cent to just under 9 per cent with the loss of around 140 000 full time jobs.

Euan Robertson from New York City's economic development team said that the then Mayor of New York, Mike Bloomberg, and his group of advisors came up with a plan to 'build a talent engine'. This was designed to stem unemployment by attracting coders and tech companies to New York (Lohr 2019).

With major financial institutions failing, there was also suddenly a large number of technically skilled analysts, information and communications technology (ICT) workers, media and business professionals who found themselves unemployed and full of ideas on ways to do things better using the new digital tools available.

It was these people with high education levels, industry experience and global networks who suddenly had the time and freedom to set up their own businesses, employing the latest technology to grow the fledgling 'Silicon Alley' cluster of tech firms in downtown Manhattan. This cluster was soon supplemented by a growing number of tech startups forming in the coffee shops of Brooklyn, where they were migrating into low-rent areas near the waterfront.

> *The city has a strong talent base that is fuelled by more than 120 universities, and in fact more than 5 million residents in the city are aged 25 and up and have at least a Bachelor's degree. NYC also had more than 7,500 computer science graduates in 2018 alone (Ludwig 2019).*

Platform-based support network Tech:nyc was formed to connect startup founders with local IT schools, venture capital and commercial opportunities.

New York City came out of recession 1–3 years before many other parts of the country. This was in part because of the Wall Street bail out deals, but it is also attributed to the rise in technology startups, jobs and income (Lohr 2019).

According to Tech:nyc, New York City's tech sector had more than 9000 startups in 2021 and in 2019 was ranked second globally for startup output. In 2021, there were 333 000 jobs in New York in the tech sector, which was valued at over $71 billion – the third most valuable technology ecosystem in the world. Brooklyn's tech hub grew over 350 per cent since 2008, and New York City is now known as the global centre for blockchain and life sciences technology innovation (Tech:nyc 2020).

Unsuccessful skills-led innovation effort: New Zealand

New Zealand is a politically stable nation known for high quality agricultural products (particularly dairy, honey and wool), adventure tourism and a fledgling but highly respected film production industry. New Zealand also attracts around 120 000 international students each year to study at its highly regarded schools, universities and tertiary training centres (New Zealand Ministry of Education – Te Tahuha O Te Matauranga 2017a).

New Zealand offers international students the opportunity to stay in the country after they complete their studies. Despite the high quality of life offered and liveability of New Zealand, the proportion of international students choosing to stay after completing their education has been declining. The number of students staying depends on their country of origin, however, with students from India staying at higher rates than students from China (New Zealand Ministry of Education - Te Tahuha O Te Matauranga 2017b).

Domestic students also have high rates of emigration once they complete their degree, and this increases with the level of qualification. Figures from 2017 showed that, after 5 years, 45 per cent of doctorate graduates and around

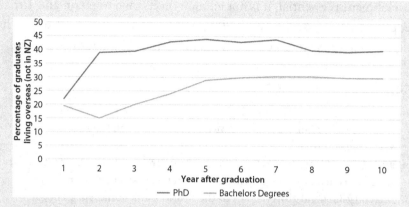

Fig. 3.4. Percentage of graduates working overseas after qualifying from higher education institutions in New Zealand, as of 2017. Source: Statistics New Zealand, recreated graph from New Zealand Ministry of Education – Te Tahuhu O Te Matauranga (2017c).

30 per cent of all Bachelor degree graduates from New Zealand universities are living and working overseas (Fig. 3.4).

The 'brain drain' of New Zealand graduates has been a concern for New Zealand policy makers for decades (New Zealand Ministry of Education – Te Tahuhu O Te Matauranga 2017c). The main reason graduates leave New Zealand is that they are offered higher wages elsewhere.

> *The Organization for Economic Cooperation and Development (OECD) estimates that almost a quarter (24.2%) of all New Zealanders with university-level educations have emigrated. Among OECD nations, only Ireland has suffered as much brain drain. ... Between 2012 and 2013, the country's researcher headcount (per million of the population) dropped by almost 11% and its ranking in the Global Innovation Index dropped four slots. Given that innovation can be a highly influential driver of competitive advantage, how can New Zealand build or maintain any advantage while losing so many of its best and brightest? (Groysberg and Bell 2013).*

Summary

Skills development is an essential component of developing an innovation hotspot and can be achieved through formal training, workplace training and local knowledge spillovers or by attracting skilled people from other areas. Skilled people are especially important for the development of knowledge-intensive and higher-value industry. But while skills development is essential, it is not enough on its own to retain and attract people; there needs to be local opportunity for them to stay. The following chapters focus on the elements that create that opportunity.

References

American Immigration Council (2017) Fact Sheet: Foreign-born STEM Workers in the United States. American Immigration Council, Washington DC.

Annan K (1997) 'If information and knowledge are central to democracy, they are conditions for development,' says Secretary-General. Address by Secretary-General Kofi Annan to the World Bank conference Global Knowledge '97, in Toronto, Canada, on 22 June. Press Release SG/SM/6268. United Nations, Geneva.

Atherton J, Bratanova A, Markey-Towler B (2020) Who is the blockchain employee? Exploring skills in demand using observations from the Australian labour market and behavioural institutional cryptoeconomics. *Journal of the British Blockchain Association* **3**, 1–12. doi:10.31585/jbba-3-2-(4)2020

Australian Bureau of Statistics (2020) One in five businesses face skills shortages. Australian Bureau of Statistics, Canberra.

Bonaccorsi A, Colombo M, Guerini M, Rossi-Lamastra C (2013) University specialization and new firm creation across industries. *Small Business Economics* **41**, 837–863. doi:10.1007/s11187-013-9509-5

Brucker H (2015) The effect of immigration on innovation and labor markets. In *Immigration Policy and the Search for Skilled Workers: A summary of a workshop.* (Eds G Cohen, A Coulthurst and J Alpa) pp. 79–93. National Academies Press, Washington DC. doi:10.17226/20145

Buzard K, Carlino GA, Hunt RM, Carr JK, Smith TE (2020) Localized knowledge spillovers: evidence from the spatial clustering of R&D labs and patent citations. *Regional Science and Urban Economics* **81**, 103490. doi:10.1016/j.regsciurbeco.2019.103490

Carlino GA, Hunt R (2009) *What explains the quantity and quality of local inventive activity? Brookings-Wharton Papers on Urban Affairs 2009.* (Eds G Burtless and JR Pack) pp. 65–123. Brookings Institution, Washington.

Carlino G, Kerr WR (2015) Agglomeration and innovation. In *Handbook of Regional and Urban Economics* vol 5. (Eds G Duranton, V Henderson and WC Strange) pp. 349–404. Elsevier BV, Amsterdam. doi.org/10.1016/B978-0-444-59517-1.00006-4

Carlino G, Hunt R, Duranton G, Weinberg BA (2009) What explains the quality and quantity of local inventive activity? In *Brookings-Wharton Papers on Urban Affairs.* (Eds G Burtless and JR Pack) pp. 65–123. Brookings Institution, Washington.

Diebolt C, Hippe R (2019) The long-run impact of human capital on innovation and economic development in the regions of Europe. *Applied Economics* **51**, 542–563. doi:10.1080/00036846.2018.1495820

Dunne C (2014) *8 Of Google's Craziest Offices.* Fast Company, San Francisco, 4 October. <https://www.fastcompany.com/3028909/8-of-googles-craziest-offices>

Faggian A, McCann P (2009) Human capital, graduate migration and innovation in British regions. *Cambridge Journal of Economics* **33**, 317–333. doi:10.1093/cje/ben042

Finnestrand HO, Magerøy K, Ravn JE (2015) More Than What Was Asked for: Company specific competence programs as innovation hothouses. In *IFIP Advances in Information and Communication Technology* vol. 459. (Editor-in-Chief K Rannenberg) pp. 399–405. Springer International Publishing, Cham, Switzerland.

Fitzsimons P (2017) Human capital theory and education. In *Encyclopedia of Educational Philosophy and Theory.* (Ed. MA Peters) pp. 29–67. Springer, Singapore.

Florida R (2003) *The Rise of the Creative Class: And how it's transforming work, leisure, community and everyday life.* Pluto Press, North Melbourne, Vic.

Florida R, Gaetani R (2020) The university's Janus face: The innovation–inequality nexus. *Managerial and Decision Economics* **41**, 1097–1112. doi:10.1002/mde.2938

Groysberg B, Bell D (2013) What boards can do about brain drain. *Harvard Business Review*, 17 December.

Gumbau-Albert M, Maudos J (2009) Patents, technological inputs and spillovers among regions. *Applied Economics* **41**, 1473–1486. doi:10.1080/00036840601032250

Hofheinz P (2009) EU 2020: why skills are key for Europe's future. *Policy Brief* **IV**, 1–23.

Hunt J, Gauthier-Loiselle M (2010) How much does immigration boost innovation? *American Economic Journal: Macroeconomics* **2**, 31–56. doi:10.1257/mac.2.2.31

Kell HJ, Lubinski D, Benbow CP, Steiger, JH (2013) Creativity and technical innovation: spatial ability's unique role. *Psychological Science* **24**, 1831–1836. doi:10.1177/0956797613478615

Kerr WR (2019a) *The Gift of Global Talent: How migration shapes business, economy & society.* Stanford Business Books, Stanford, California.

Kerr WR (2019b) The gift of global talent: innovation policy and the economy. Working Paper 25875. National Bureau of Economic Research, Cambridge, Massachusetts.

Lin J (2011) Technological adaptation, cities and new work. *The Review of Economics and Statistics* **93**, 554–574. doi:10.1162/REST_a_00079

Lohr S (2019) It started with a jolt: how New York became a tech town. *The New York Times*, New York, 22 February.

Ludwig S (2019) *How New York City's Startups Have Become a Global Force*. Startup Genome, New York.

Marginson S (2019) Limitations of human capital theory. *Studies in Higher Education* **44**, 287–301. doi:10.1080/03075079.2017.1359823

Marr B (2018) 7 skills of the future (that AIs and robots can't do better than humans). *Forbes*, Jersey City NJ, 6 August. <https://www.forbes.com/sites/bernardmarr/2018/08/06/7-job-skills-of-the-future-that-ais-and-robots-cant-do-better-than-humans/?sh=9a7054e6c2e9>

McGuirk H, Lenihan H, Hart M (2015) Measuring the impact of innovative human capital on small firms' propensity to innovate. *Research Policy* **44**, 965–976. doi:10.1016/j.respol.2014.11.008

National Academies of Science Engineering and Medicine (2015) The effect of immigration on innovation and labor markets. In *Immigration Policy and the Search for Skilled Workers: A summary of a workshop*. (Eds G Cohen, A Coulthurst and J Alpa) pp. 79–96. National Academies Press, Washington. doi:10.17226/20145

New York State Labor Department (2020) *Labor Data Overview*. New York State Labor Department, New York.

New Zealand Ministry of Education – Te Tahuhu O Te Matauranga (2017a) Export Education Levy Annual Report. Ministry of Education NZ, Wellington. <https://www.educationcounts.govt.nz/__data/assets/pdf_file/0008/183977/Export-Education-Levy-Annual-Report-2016-2017.pdf>

New Zealand Ministry of Education – Te Tahuhu O Te Matauranga (2017b) Moving places: Destinations and earnings of international graduates. Ministry of Education NZ, Wellington. <https://www.educationcounts.govt.nz/publications/tertiary_education/education-outcomes/destinations/moving-places-destinations-and-earnings-of-international-graduates>

New Zealand Ministry of Education – Te Tahuhu O Te Matauranga (2017c) Factsheet: Young, domestic graduate outcomes – destinations. Ministry of Education NZ, Wellington <https://www.educationcounts.govt.nz/__data/assets/pdf_file/0009/183591/Young,-international-graduate-outcomes-destinations-factsheet-December-2017b.pdf>

OECD (2011) *Skills for Innovation and Research*. OECD Publishing, Paris.

Pugh O'Mara M (2005) *Cities of Knowledge: Cold war science and the search for the next Silicon Valley.* Princeton University Press, Princeton.

Quiggin J (1999) Human capital theory and education policy in Australia. *The Australian Economic Review* **32**, 130–144. doi:10.1111/1467-8462.00100

Rabiul Islam MD, Ang JB, Madsen JB (2014) Quality-adjusted human capital and productivity growth. *Economic Inquiry* **52**, 757–777. doi:10.1111/ecin.12052

Ramos R, Suriñach J, Artís M (2010) Human capital spillovers, productivity and regional convergence in Spain: human capital spillovers, productivity and convergence. *Papers in Regional Science* **89**, 435–447. doi:10.1111/j.1435-5957.2010.00296.x

Santa M, Stojkoski V, Josimovski M, Trpevski I, Kocarev L (2019) Robust determinants of companies' capacity to innovate: a Bayesian model averaging approach. *Technology Analysis and Strategic Management* **31**, 1283–1296. doi:10.1080/09537325.2019.1605052

Saxenian A (1996) *Regional Advantage: Culture and competition in Silicon Valley and Route 128.* Harvard University Press, Cambridge, Massachusetts.

Simonsson J (2021) Anticipation through collaboration and capabilities. In *Anticipatory Governance – International Peer Workshop.* Paris, 12 March. OECD and Sweden's Committee for technological innovation and ethics.

Smith A, Courvisanos J, Tuck J, McEachern S (2012) Building the capacity to innovate: the role of human capital. National Vocational Education and Training Research and Evaluation Program Research Report. National Centre for Vocational and Educational Research (NCVER), Adelaide.

Startup Muster (2018) Startup Muster Annual Report. < https://www.austcyber.com/tools-and-resources/2018-startup-muster-annual-report>

Taylor HA, Hutton A (2013) Think3d!: Training spatial thinking fundamental to STEM education. *Cognition and Instruction* **31**, 434–455. doi:10.1080/07370008.2013.828727

Tech:nyc (2020) *NYC Tech Ecosystem Overview.* Tech:nyc, New York.

The Economist (2017) Shenzen is a hothouse of innovation: the copycats are out, innovators are in. *The Economist*, London, 6 April.

Universities Australia (2020) 2020 Higher Education Facts and Figures. Universities Australia, Canberra.

US Bureau of Labor Statistics (2020) *Foreign-born workers made up 17.4 percent of labor force in 2019.* Bureau of Labor Statistics, Washington DC.

US Department of Defense (2020) Fiscal year 2020. Industrial capabilities report to Congress. Department of Defense, Washington DC.

Valero A, Van Reenen J (2016) The economic impact of universities: evidence from across the globe. NBER Working Paper 22501. National Bureau of Economic Research (NBER), Cambridge, Massachusetts.

Vandenbussche J, Aghion P, Meghir C (2006) Growth, distance to frontier and composition of human capital. *Journal of Economic Growth* **11**, 97–127. doi:10.1007/s10887-006-9002-y

World Bank (2020) The Human Capital Index 2020 Update: Human capital in the time of COVID-19. World Bank, Washington DC.

World Economic Forum (2020) The Future of Jobs Report 2020. World Economic Forum, Cologny, Switzerland.

4

Mission-led innovation

Aim

To solve large societal problems through defining goals for innovative and technological effort

Mission-led innovation is where a government or organisation sets goals or targets as an inducement or incentive for technological development, investment, collaboration or industrial change. It is also referred to as challenge-led, mission-oriented or goal-driven innovation.

The original moonshot

During the Second World War, the German military developed the world's first long-range ballistic missiles: the V-2 rockets. At the end of the war, in 1945, the technology was replicated by scientists in the US, USSR and UK. German scientists who had worked on the V-2 rockets were recruited to both the US and USSR military to further develop their range and carrying capacity. The weaponry that had ended the Second World War – the nuclear bomb – was also being developed by all three military forces. The idea of nuclear bombs on the heads of long-range ballistic missiles began to reshape the geopolitical landscape from 1945 onwards. Along with the need for eye-in-the-sky surveillance and detection systems, the need for an advantage in the deployment of new bombs and missiles began the Cold War and the Space Race between the US and the USSR (Kell *et al.* 2013; Launius 2019).

In the 15 years following the end of the war, the US government watched as the Soviet rocket and space program achieved some impressive feats: they developed hybrid fuel and unique rocket stabilising systems, introduced a multistage propulsion system essential for piercing through the outer atmosphere into space, and in 1957 they successfully put the first satellites (Sputniks 1 and 2) into orbit around Earth. Even though the US soon followed in putting a satellite into space in 1959 (despite several high-profile, humiliating failures), the Soviets were then again the first to put a person into space, Yuri Gagarin in 1961, and bring him safely back to Earth after a complete orbit.

Being second place to the USSR in the development of space and rocket technology started to become a political issue. The American public were unsettled by the idea that the Soviets could see or hear them from space, and possibly launch intercontinental ballistic nuclear warheads from Earth or satellite bases. When President John F Kennedy was elected at the end of 1960, he was determined to get back into first place in the space race and restore public confidence. But to do that, he had to gain significant funding and public support for the newly established National Aeronautics and Space Administration (NASA). So, he set his country a seemingly impossible but heroic challenge: to put a man on the moon by the end of the decade and bring him back safely to Earth. The significance of this challenge was that it was extremely risky – the technology did not yet exist and it was long term (beyond even the term of his elected government). It was also a challenge that could only be undertaken at enormous cost and would need to marshal talents from several fields. But as President Kennedy said (in a speech to Congress, 25 May 1961):

> I believe we possess all the resources and talents necessary. But the facts of the matter are that we have never made the national decisions or marshaled the national resources required for such leadership. We have never specified long-range goals on an urgent time schedule, or managed our resources and our time so as to insure their fulfillment...
>
> I believe that this nation should commit itself to achieving the goal, before this decade is out, of landing a man on the moon and returning him safely to the Earth.

Fig. 4.1.   Astronaut Buzz Aldrin on the Apollo 11 mission, beside the US flag planted on the first moon landing, 20 July 1969. Public domain image by NASA.

As history attests, the challenge to send a man safely to the moon and back was achieved in 1969 – just before the end of the decade (Fig. 4.1).

The challenge set by Kennedy saw the US government dedicate over $28 billion in funds ($283 billion adjusted for inflation to 2020 figures) to the lunar missions between 1960 and 1973 (Planetary Society 2020). Along the way, thousands of space technologies were developed that had terrestrial and commercial applications in such fields as communications, geolocation, materials, robotics, food science, electronics, energy, medical devices and computing. The challenge issued by President Kennedy in 1961, who sadly did not live to see it achieved, became known as 'a moonshot', and it is the basis of mission-led innovation. It was the goal, the vision, the glory of putting a person on the moon that stimulated the innovation effort, including gaining the public support and the long-term commitment of large sums of public funds that would allow it to happen.

Getting to the moon wasn't the first scientific mission

Although the moonshot is the best known and most widely cited example of mission-led innovation, it certainly wasn't the first. The challenge to build world-leading engineering and scientific marvels that progressed technology and inspired innovative effort were a feature of world fairs. Starting with the Great Exhibition in London in 1851, world fairs were competitions that resulted in awe-inspiring structures such as Crystal Palace in London, which used and progressed the technologies of plate glass manufacture, cast-iron architecture and ventilation. Similarly, the Eiffel Tower (1889) (Fig. 4.2) and the Chicago Ferris Wheel (1893), which at 80 m tall was the largest single forged cast iron and steel structure in the world at that time, both led to patents in precision engineering and construction techniques.

The US military were one of the first organisations to issue technological specifications for equipment that did not yet exist. During the First and Second World Wars, the US Navy's Bureau of Steam Engineering was nurturing relationships with inventors and

Fig. 4.2. Eiffel Tower under construction before the 1889 World Fair. Public domain image.

pioneers in energy, radio, electronics and engineering. Inventors and holders of new patents were invited to demonstrate their wares to the navy, who would then push the science ahead by issuing specifications for improved designs and functionality of the existing technologies. Those specifications were for equipment such as radios that could reach further, communicate with submarines and block out interfering signals. These technical challenges evolved into formal challenges issued through the Defense Advanced Research Projects Agency (DARPA) and the National Aeronautics and Space Administration (NASA). These challenges still incentivise innovation today (Dubois 2003; Orlowski 2015). Since the original moonshot, governments have issued challenges or set targets in a range of fields.

Mariana Mazzucato and the modern mission

One of the most fervent and influential advocates of modern mission-led innovation is University College London Professor and economist Mariana Mazzucato (Fig. 4.3). Mazzucato describes the evolution of mission-led innovation from purely technical challenges – such as developing the technology to put a person on the moon – to social challenges or 'wicked problems' – such as solving global climate change, reducing poverty or global inequality. These problems are broad and require long-term planning, and they cross sectors, disciplines and borders.

Mazzucato suggests that missions create new markets and new industries through incentivising innovation. Smart people like to be challenged and to flex their intellect, so they are drawn to the challenge

Fig. 4.3. Professor Mariana Mazzucato. Image by Simon Fraser University – Communications & Marketing is licenced under CC BY 2.0.

model, which also serves to forge collaboration and trust between actors who work towards a common goal. Mazzucato states that innovation is given a direction through a mission, and by applying innovation to societal problems, innovation-led growth can be more sustainable and equitable (Mazzucato 2015, 2019).

The use of missions to communicate directionality of change or progress, however, is not particularly new. Companies have been using 'mission statements' since at least 1973, when business management writer Peter Drucker suggested that it is a company's mission that defines it (Drucker 1973). The use of corporate mission statements became standard management practice from the 1980s onwards. Mission statements are used to communicate a corporation's aim, ambition and possibly their values, expertise, and scope of operations to both customers and employees. For instance, Google's mission statement is: 'Our company mission is to organise the world's information and make it universally accessible and useful' (Google 2021).

Intermediate 'big hairy audacious goals' for company teams or departments have also become common in the development of company or program strategy as a way to motivate and galvanise innovative effort.

Adding a competitive element

A mission will usually set the direction for change, while targets involved in many missions introduce a quantity or degree of change so mission managers can assess progress. The addition of a competitive element to reach the mission is sometimes added to open up the mission to as many innovative players as possible.

Researchers, inventors or companies are then asked to enter into competitions, pitches, hackathons or competitive assessments in order to gain support in the form of funds, commercialisation advice or co-development opportunities. Mission-led funding is sometimes attached to incubator or accelerator services, which seek to support or harvest new ideas from new actors. These may include startups, young or new industry players or small business. Accelerators then help them commercialise their products in achieving the mission's aim. In some cases, challenges are part of more open innovation development, such as Open Data initiatives, use of government infrastructure or cooperative research and development (R&D) arrangements.

In this, there has been a growing number of science, industry and development agencies adopting a missions or a challenge approach to the allocation of innovation funds. Agencies that have introduced new and competitive mission-led funds for innovation since 2016 include the UK's Industrial Strategy Challenge Fund (UK Research and Innovation 2017), Horizon Europe's missions (Cahill 2020) and Australia's CSIRO Challenges and Mission program (CSIRO 2021). Organisations such as the UK's National Endowment for Science, Technology and the Arts (NESTA) are calling for public R&D funds to be:

> more mission-driven, more focused on bringing new ideas into the real world, more devolved and more accountable.
>
> … the public wants to see innovation spending tackling societal challenges: climate change, inequality and poor health. The Government now needs to show how it will align this significant investment with these priorities. NESTA believes that a greater proportion of the R&D budget should be mission-driven, rather than purely curiosity-driven (Gabriel 2020).

A global mission to reduce carbon emissions and transition to renewable energy sources is the inspiration for an international initiative, Mission Innovation, that has issued competitive technological challenges to double investment in clean energy R&D. Mission Innovation has support from 25 member countries and the European Commission, as well as backing from global institutions including the World Bank, World Economic Forum and the International Renewable Energy Agency (IRENA).

Not all missions go to plan or result in successful outcomes, however. The OECD's Observatory for Public Sector Innovation suggests that for a mission to be successful it must:

- create meaningful change
- have a clear or explicit outcome
- have a good system of tracking to show if progress is being made to achieve the mission

- appeal to a cultivated ecosystem of innovative partners
- be ambitious (Roberts 2018).

In many ways, applying missions to 'wicked problems' is a rebranding of the innovation budgets of government departments: the mission of the Department of Health is to create a healthier population, the mission of the Department of Defence is to protect citizens against foreign attacks, the mission for the Department of Education is to improve the skills and qualifications of citizens. Competitive tenders for government work to meet these missions don't necessarily involve innovation or meet certain targets, although many government departments apply targets to specific program outcomes. Issues such as climate change or energy transition are increasingly in their own government departments, or policy to achieve these goals may form across departments.

There are some challenges for which a technological response is almost implicit and the desired outcome is obvious. For example, the use of technology in warfare is to create superior weaponry that will provide an asymmetric military advantage with the desired outcome being to win the war. For instance, the Soviet military were the first to develop manned spacecraft without an explicit, publicly stated mission to be the first to put a man into orbit. Their 'moonshot' was implicit in their research effort. In the response to a global pandemic, which involves developing new vaccines, societal responses or treatments, the desired outcome is to eradicate the pathogen or at least significantly reduce the threat to human life and burden on society.

Overcoming the short-term-ness of democratic nations

One of the big advantages of mission-led innovation is that it can help overcome the problem of innovation funding being allocated by short-term, democratically elected governments. Achieving innovative goals can take a lot longer than the term of one government, such as Kennedy's moonshot innovation effort, which took place over three US presidencies, those of Kennedy, Johnson and Nixon. The goal of curbing climate change will take decades and global cooperation, and the goal of many national governments to transform economies from low income to high income can take 40 years or more. Mission-led innovation has the potential to garner the public support needed for large funding allocations over the longer term.

Many mainly communist and socialist nations have achieved sustained economic growth by setting five-year plans and goals. Russia was the first country to set a five-year plan for economic growth and transformation in 1928, and countries such as China, Vietnam and Bhutan followed and still create five-year plans for economic, social and technological change. Up until 1996, South Korea used five-year plans to assist in developing the economy from one based on agricultural commodities to one based on high-technology fields such as microelectronics, computing hardware, cars, bioengineering, materials sciences and aerospace. Creating goals and targets kept the innovation effort focused and assured resourcing over sustained periods.

Missions can provide a focus for innovation, but there are several reasons to be cautious in their application.

- **The mission can be too narrowly focused on one societal goal at the expense of others.** For instance, improving food production may neglect environmental conditions and constraints.
- **The mission may be too vague or ill-defined to be meaningful or effective.** For instance, a mission to improve population happiness by a certain date may not take into consideration economic or demographic changes during that time or cater for the wellbeing of all population subgroups.
- **The mission may have unintended consequences through inappropriate measurement.** Performance targets are widely used in missions and general management practice, but some have been shown to have unintended consequences or distort practices in order to achieve a higher level of progress against targets. For example, when reducing waiting times in British hospitals was made a goal of the National Health Service (NHS)

in 2000 (with 'waiting time' defined as the time it took for someone to be assessed by a medical professional), many hospitals employed a 'hello nurse' to make contact with a patient shortly after they entered the hospital. The 'hello nurse' gave them a quick triage assessment before leaving people to wait for hours to be treated by a doctor. Not only were people waiting just as long to be treated, resources were being diverted from providing that treatment (Mannion and Braithwaite 2012).

- **The mission that focuses innovators on change may also galvanise and activate resistance.** For instance, missions that move towards clean energy targets may activate and galvanise the fossil fuel sector and cause companies in that sector to invest in burning and selling more fossil fuels while the market still allows it, thereby counteracting the clean energy outcomes.

- **Missions may not be achieved, leaving the political actors or managers behind them to look like failures.** If NASA had not achieved its goal of landing a man on the moon by the end of the decade, or if the Apollo missions had ended in tragedy, there may have been political consequences for NASA or the political interests supporting budget allocations to fund the missions. Politicians and funding agencies can be shy to sign up to missions with explicit targets and timeframes, particularly if/ when the mission relies on undeveloped technology.

- **Missions need to be attached to healthy, long-term funding sources.** The broader missions or grand challenges to solve large, wicked societal problems are not short-term. They are likely to take many years to produce outcomes and involve technological and political reform. Many goals may not be able to be completed in one political term and this is off-putting for many governments. This puts the outcome of many missions at risk, or places the mission at risk of becoming irrelevant over time.

- **Competitive processes attached to missions may be too time-consuming and costly.** Participating in missions or competitions may be too costly for many startups or technology developers, or may involve divulging unprotected intellectual property (IP), concepts or ideas before there is secure funding in place to develop them.

- **There is immense value in blue-sky or basic research.** In the face of an increasing amount of funding tied to agendas or missions, there have been calls for respect and continued funding for 'blue-sky' or curiosity-driven research that does not have an obvious or immediate benefit or return on investment (Shurlock 2014; Skoglund 2015; Kwon 2017; Goymann 2019). Some of the largest breakthroughs in science have come from investigating strange and inexplicable phenomena or following up confounding but failed research experiments. This includes breakthroughs that led to antibiotics, magnetic resonance imaging (MRI) and wifi, and the discovery of radioactive elements, gravitational waves, and the structure of DNA, and the manipulation of mRNA vital for the development of the new breed of vaccines. Without the freedom and funding to investigate and discover new phenomena or applications unrelated to a particular agenda, these breakthroughs may never have occurred.

Table 4.1. Advantages and disadvantages of mission-led innovation efforts

Advantages	Disadvantages
• Missions can bring together actors and researchers from across departments, countries and agencies. • Missions can incentivise long-term investment in innovation through galvanising public support and trust and creating a vision for the future. • Missions can inspire achievement through competitive pressures if linked to competitive funding pools or if progress towards the goal is tracked across various parties/countries. • Missions can provide directionality to R&D funding, rather than just investing in blue sky or curiosity-based research.	• Missions that are too vague or broad, don't set targets or timeframes, or that aren't properly resourced may not achieve the desired outcomes. • Missions that are too narrow or that only achieve the target outcomes at the expense of other areas may not galvanise broad support from across an ecosystem of researchers. Targets for missions may also have unintended consequences or encourage a 'gaming' of the system for continued funding. • Mission competitions may be too costly for many innovative players to participate in and require too much public funding over the long term to be politically attractive. • Missions with strict timeframes and targets may fail and embarrass political leaders. • Blue-sky basic research (as opposed to applied or mission-based research) has led to significant breakthrough discoveries that have progressed technology or scientific understanding.

Successful mission-led innovation: The Coalition for Epidemic Preparedness Innovations (CEPI)

The Coalition for Epidemic Preparedness Innovations (CEPI) is a mission-based global coalition of public, private and non-government organisations coordinating responses to emerging infectious diseases.

The mission of CEPI is to:

Stimulate and accelerate the development of vaccines against emerging infectious diseases and enable access to these vaccines for people during outbreaks (Coalition for Epidemic Preparedness Innovations 2021).

CEPI was formed in 2017 to develop vaccines to stop future pandemics. After efforts to control an Ebola outbreak in West Africa in 2013–16 were unnecessarily stymied by corporate and national interests, scientists came together to form a global coalition to fund, develop and control distribution of new vaccines. Emerging pathogens do not stop at borders and can have devastating social and economic consequences even in small outbreaks. The West African Ebola outbreak killed over 11 000 people in five countries and disrupted local economies and livelihoods for over 3 years. The global COVID-19 pandemic cost an estimated 5 per cent of global gross domestic product in 2020. Vaccine development is also costly, and vaccines need to be delivered internationally based on need, not national interests, for disease outbreaks to be effectively controlled (Fig. 4.4).

Just 2 years after it had formed in 2017, CEPI had mobilised more than $750 million from a range of sources (national governments, international bodies and large philanthropic funds), to support the development of novel vaccines (Gouglas *et al.* 2019). In 2020, an additional US$1.5 billion was committed to CEPI's work and CEPI had entered into research partnerships to assist in the development of over 20 vaccines for priority pathogens. Most of these vaccines have been developed for pathogen outbreaks in lower- and middle-income countries that do not have the resources to develop vaccines themselves.

During the COVID-19 pandemic, CEPI was one of the first organisations to begin the development of a vaccine in early 2020 after the genetic sequence of the virus was known. CEPI had already dedicated US$50 million to development of vaccine platform technologies for rapid, collaborative and global vaccine development. These platforms were pivoted and used by platform partners around the world to rapidly develop 11 potential COVID-19 vaccines. By the end of 2020, two of those vaccines had sufficiently demonstrated efficacy and safety in human and animal trials to start vaccine manufacture and roll-out. CEPI also assisted in funding the manufacture, testing and rollout of vaccines.

Fig. 4.4. Scientists at CSIRO's Australian Centre for Disease Preparedness work on COVID-19 vaccine trials, results of which are shared with CEPI as part of the global effort for vaccine development. Image by CSIRO, Australia's national science agency.

> *CEPI has invested in one of the world's largest portfolio of vaccines against COVID-19 which continues to grow and be strengthened during the start of 2021, has awarded forgivable loans in 2020 to expand global manufacturing capacity, has established a global network of laboratories to standardise vaccine assessment, and has emerging viral strains on vaccine effectiveness (Coalition for Epidemic Preparedness Innovations 2020).*

The fact that a ready-to-administer vaccine had been developed within 12 months was a global first. The fastest a vaccine had been developed before this was the mumps vaccine in the 1960s, which took 4 years. By creating global platforms and utilising skills and capacity from scientific bodies, manufacturing facilities and vaccine delivery partners from around the world, CEPI was instrumental in shortening the duration of the COVID-19 pandemic and saved millions of lives. CEPI was also a key partner in the COVAX scheme, which has provided access to COVID-19 vaccines to frontline workers and high-risk and vulnerable groups in lower and middle-income countries.

In 2021, CEPI was seeking US$3.5 billion over 5 years to further develop its capacity to 'eliminate the threat of epidemics and pandemics'. This investment, effort and remarkable achievement would not have occurred without the coalescence of support around its mission.

Less successful mission-led innovation effort: UK missed biodiversity targets

In 2010, the UK government signed up to the global Convention on Biological Diversity. Its mission: to protect Earth's biodiversity and prevent species extinction.

In signing the Convention, the UK agreed to work towards and report on 19 targets across five overarching goals:

1. Address the underlying causes of biodiversity.
2. Promote sustainable use of natural resources and habitats.
3. Safeguard ecosystems, species and genetic diversity.
4. Enhance the benefits to all diversity and ecosystems.
5. Implement planning, knowledge management and capacity building.

To meet the 19 targets, the UK government stated they would gather evidence through the development of indicators, research, pilot projects and knowledge exchange.

A 2019 report from the UK's Joint National Conservation Committee (2019) found that the UK government had not met, and was making insufficient

Fig. 4.5. The Turtle Dove (*Streptopelia turtur*), once common in the UK, has declined by 94 per cent since 1995 in the UK and by 78 per cent across Europe. It is now listed as endangered by the International Union for the Conservation of Nature (IUCN). Photo: Andy Morffew from Itchen Abbas, Hampshire, UK, is licenced under CC BY 2.0.

progress on, 14 out of their 19 targets. An increase in pollution, degrading fish stocks, low public awareness and declines in woodland, farmland and marine biodiversity were all highlighted by the targets that were missed. Public funding to protect the environment and habitats had fallen in the UK by 17 per cent over 5 years, and there were worrying declines in pollinating insects. Internationally, the UK was assessed as having an insufficient rate of progress towards achieving the targets and thus the overall mission of protecting biodiversity.

Despite not meeting 14 of its 19 stated targets, there were several positive actions mentioned that promoted innovation: citizen science projects and intergovernmental platforms, agri-environmental schemes on farmlands, reintroduction programs and environmental publications on environmental monitoring.

The positives, however, were not enough for the UK government to avoid widespread criticism for its environmental record as a consequence of signing onto the Convention, although globally the program itself may be stimulating considerable innovation in protecting, or at least efforts in monitoring, threatened species (Fig. 4.5).

Summary

Missions can be an effective way of steering, promoting and incentivising participation and investment in an innovation agenda, but they can have pitfalls that need to be carefully avoided. Unintended consequences, humiliating missed targets, long-term costs and the crowding out of productive blue-sky research are some of the reasons why missions need thoughtful, well-resourced design and management. The resourcing of innovation is the subject of the next chapter.

References

Cahill M (2020) *Horizon Europe – the next research and innovation framework programme 2021–2027.* Horizon Europe and Enterprise Ireland, Dublin.
Coalition for Epidemic Preparedness Innovationa (CEPI) (2020) CEPI Annual Report 2020. CEPI, London.
Coalition for Epidemic Preparedness Innovations (2021) *Creating a world in which epidemics are no longer a threat to humanity: Our Mission.* CEPI, Olso, Norway. <https://cepi.net/about/whyweexist/>
CSIRO (2021) *Mission-driven science.* Australian Government, Canberra. <https://www.csiro.au/en/about/challenges-missions>

Drucker P (1973) *Management: Tasks, responsibilities, practices.* Harper & Row, New York.

Dubois L (2003) DARPA's approach to innovation and its reflection in industry, in reducing the time from basic research to innovation in the chemical sciences: A workshop report to the Chemical Sciences Roundtable. National Research Council (US) Chemical Sciences Roundtable, Washington DC.

Gabriel M (2020) NESTA responds to Budget 2020. NESTA, London.

Google (2021) *About.* Google, Mountain View, California. <https://about.google/>

Gouglas D, Christodoulou M, Plotkin S, Hatchett R (2019) CEPI: Driving progress toward epidemic preparedness and response. *American Journal of Epidemiology* **41**, 28–33. doi:10.1093/epirev/mxz012

Goymann W (2019) Editorial: On the importance of studying animal behaviour – or any other kind of 'blue sky' research. *Ethology* **125**, 501–502. doi:10.1111/eth.12920

Joint National Conservation Committee (2019) *Sixth National Report to the United Nations Convention on Biological Diversity: United Kingdom of Great Britain and Northern Ireland.* JNCC, Peterborough. <https://www.cbd.int/doc/nr/nr-06/gb-nr-06-p1-en.pdf>

Kell HJ, Lubinksi D, Benbow CP, Steiger JH (2013) Creativity and technical innovation: spatial ability's unique role. *Psychological Science* **24**, 1831–1836. doi:10.1177/0956797613478615

Kwon D (2017) How blue sky research shapes the future. *Symmetry: Dimensions of particle physics.* 18 April. <https://www.symmetrymagazine.org/article/how-blue-sky-research-shapes-the-future>

Launius RD (2019) *Reaching for the Moon: A short history of the space race.* Yale University Press, New Haven.

Mannion R, Braithwaite J (2012) Unintended consequences of performance measurement in healthcare: 20 salutary lessons from the English National Health Service. *Internal Medicine Journal* **42**, 569–574. doi:10.1111/j.1445-5994.2012.02766.x

Mazzucato M (2015) How to make 'smart' innovation-led growth also 'inclusive' growth. In *New Perspectives on Industrial Policy for a Modern Britain.* (Eds D Bailey, K Cowling, PR Tomlinson.) pp. 170–180. Oxford University Press, Oxford.

Mazzucato M (2019) *Governing Missions in the European Union.* European Union, Brussells.

Orlowski MC (2015) *DARPA Robotics Challenge (DRC) (Archived).* Defense Advanced Research Projects Agency. <https://www.darpa.mil/program/darpa-robotics-challenge>

Planetary Society (2020) *How Much did the Apollo Program Cost?* The Planetary Society, Pasadena, California. <https://www.planetary.org/space-policy/cost-of-apollo>

Roberts A (2018) *Innovation Facets Part 4: Mission-oriented innovation.* OECD Observatory for Public Sector Innovation, Paris.

Shurlock B (2014) Translational research and 'blue skies' mentality brings rewards. *European Heart Journal* **35**, 2197–2198. doi:10.1093/eurheartj/ehu270

Skoglund A (2015) Climate social science – any future for 'blue sky research' in management studies? *Scandinavian Journal of Management* **31**, 147–157. doi:10.1016/j.scaman.2014.10.004

UK Research and Innovation (2017) Industrial Strategy Challenge Fund. UK Government, London.

5

Research and development and finance-led innovation

Aim

To increase innovation through the availability of dedicated funding for R&D and commercialisation

As argued in the previous chapters, innovation is expensive and risky. For every profitable innovation created, there are many, many that fail. The art of investing well in innovative ventures is only acquired with deep knowledge of both the market and technology. All governments know, however, that generating the risk-taking funds for all the attempts at innovation – both profitable and non-profitable – is critical to the development of new industries, productivity and economic growth. Funds act as an attractor, an enabler and a booster of innovation.

Research and development (R&D), corporate finance and venture capital are viewed as an innovation input – listed alongside other inputs such as human capital, business sophistication and information and communications technology (ICT) infrastructure on innovation scores (Cornell University *et al.* 2020). R&D funding generally finances an innovation from the seed of an idea to the prototyping and testing phase, while venture and corporate capital or private equity funds take the new product, process or system to market via a business or company. Venture capital is particularly important for the development of new products and companies and fuels entrepreneurialism, particularly in digital and high-tech industries. In certain industries, however, ideas can be pitched directly to

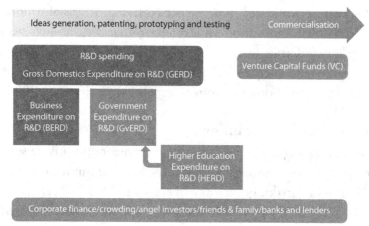

Fig. 5.1. Funding ideas to market products.

investors and venture capital firms without a lot of initial product testing. See Fig. 5.1.

Sources of innovation finance

The 2020 Global Innovation Index report was titled 'Who will finance innovation?' after the authors observed that the COVID-19 pandemic had accelerated a trend towards fewer available funds for innovative ventures:

> [M]oney to fund innovative ventures is drying up. VC [venture capital] deals are in sharp decline across North America, Asia, and Europe. There are few initial public offerings (IPOs) in sight, and the start-ups that survive may grow less attractive to – and profitable for – venture capitalists, as exit strategies such as IPOs are compromised in 2020 (Cornell University *et al.* 2020, p. xix).

While funds had dried up before and during the pandemic, changed conditions, the sudden downturn in markets and the need for renewed productivity may also stimulate innovation funding, particularly from the public sector through economic stimulus packages. The pandemic may also redirect a lot of innovation finance towards online education, health, big data, e-commerce and robotics, a consequence of the sudden need for remote work and more dispersed living. It was also noted in the 2020 Global Innovation Index report that well-known venture capital magnets (cities in India, China, the UK, the US, Israel and Luxembourg) were likely to bounce back from the economic hit of the pandemic faster than other regions (Cornell University *et al.* 2020).

Sources of funding for innovation

Innovation funding comes from both government and private sources. Government funding usually supports the areas of innovation that are high risk and loss-making, such as early stage and basic R&D (Fig. 5.2), while the private sector is more likely to support the development of

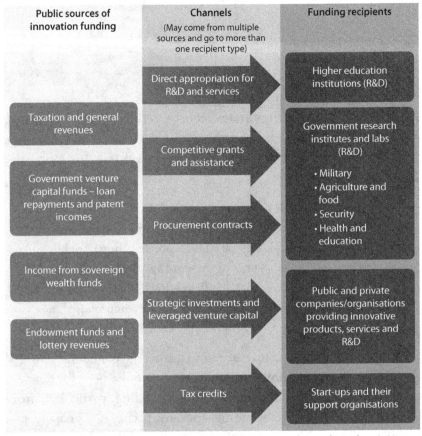

Fig. 5.2. Government funding for innovation: sources, channels and recipients (countries will differ).

applied R&D and the commercialisation of intellectual property (IP) once it has shown market potential (Fig. 5.3).

In many ways, early stage or basic R&D is considered to be an externality of a healthy economy, and one generally accepted by governments, who pour up to 5 per cent of their GDP into research and development (World Bank 2020). Many of the profits of that R&D spending are exploited by the private sector. The private sector, in turn, contributes back to the economy and the government by providing employment, taxes and higher levels of overall productivity and industry competitiveness.

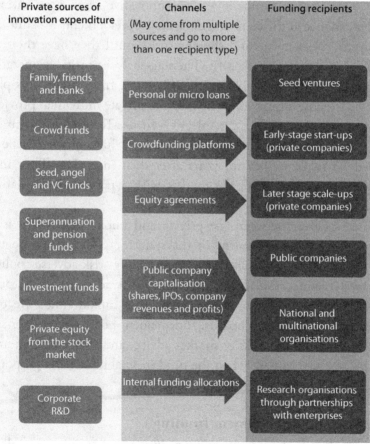

Fig. 5.3. Private sources of funding for innovation: sources, channels and recipients.

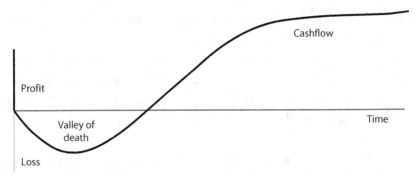

Fig. 5.4. Funding is critical through the valley of death, although this is the riskiest time to invest.

New business startups based on innovative ideas need different levels of finance at different stages in their development. Most notably they need investors to fund the enterprise until they have their first customer, and then turn a profit. The stage before profitable operations is often called 'the valley of death' (Fig. 5.4). Investors in this phase could be friends, family, angel investors (a private individual providing seed funding), or venture capital (VC) firms. Technology firms that pursue a winner-takes-all strategy through high-growth scale-ups often don't make money for years after their inception. They invest heavily early to dominate the market with a network or a platform (Srinivasan 2021).

The crossover between the private and public investment is not always clear, and low returns to the state for public investments in R&D are often questioned in traditionally risk-adverse political processes (Ejermo *et al.* 2011). Due to the risk-adversity of the public sector, publicly funded or leveraged venture capital funds are often placed with independent boards. Independent boards can better assist young firms with business or market advice, and they create an arms-length from government when the fund inevitably makes a proportion of bad investments.

Research and development funding

R&D funding is the largest source of innovation funding globally. In 2020, an estimated $2.4 trillion was invested globally in R&D by governments and industry (Heney 2020). There are many early studies that link levels of R&D investment with higher, economy-wide growth in the long run and, in particular, with improvements in total factor productivity, a type of productivity that includes efficiency improvements resulting from technological change (Romer 1990; Howitt and Aghion 1998; Zachariadis 2003; Liu 2016). Most of this research has been in endogenous growth economics, and in modelling the Schumpeterian processes of new technology and its impact on older firms through creative destruction.

As the economics has matured, there have been provisos placed on the conditions in which R&D investment contributes to long-run growth. The relationship of R&D investment to economic growth is not linear (Pessoa 2010) and, like many things, is highly contextual:

- **R&D investment drives greater economic growth in higher income countries,** as new-to-the-world innovation becomes one of the few channels to push further growth. Lower-income and developing countries better assist their GDP growth by capital investments in new equipment and infrastructure rather than in R&D. At lower stages in development, foreign direct investment (FDI) has far greater impact on economic growth than R&D expenditure (Liu 2016).

- **R&D investment drives greater innovation and growth in larger-market OECD countries.** 'Large market' OECD countries increase their innovation levels by investing more in R&D. The remaining OECD countries seemed to promote their innovation levels by adopting technology of the other OECD countries. In large-market OECD countries (which included all of the G7, Australia, the Netherlands. Spain and Switzerland), a 1.0 per cent increase in R&D will increase innovation by ~0.2 per cent. This was not seen in other OECD countries or non-OECD countries (Sylwester 2001; Ulku 2004, 2007). Another study also found R&D only contributed to GDP growth in large OECD countries; there was no clear association found in smaller OECD countries (Sylwester 2001).

- **R&D investment may have diminished returns in high-growth sectors.** In what became known as 'the Swedish paradox', researchers pointed out that Sweden had very high investment in R&D and yet reducing GDP growth. This 'paradox' was later found to be restricted to just the high-growth sectors rather than the entire economy. In the high-growth sectors, profits were reinvested in R&D. Therefore, growth in these sectors, while still substantial, had not kept pace with R&D growth. There had been diminishing, but still highly valuable, returns on investment (Ejermo *et al.* 2011).

R&D intensity goals: more aspirational than achievable

To unlock innovation and its subsequent effects on GDP growth, in the 1960s and 1970s many OECD countries set goals for their levels of R&D spending. R&D goals at around 3 per cent of gross national product (GNP) were often used, as this was the R&D expenditure of the US at the time. Nearly 50 years on, R&D intensity goals still seem to be popular. In the last 20 years, the EU, UN, OECD and UNESCO have all encouraged setting R&D intensity goals. Governments have also been keen to do so, often using their goal to tout policies towards high-tech industry or encourage corporations to undertake more R&D. As (Carvalho 2018) shows, however, very few governments have ever actually reached their R&D intensity goals, mainly because they include business expenditure on R&D (BERD) and rely on certain levels of GDP growth, both of which are relatively unpredictable.

> It is paradoxical that the complete lack of effectiveness in achieving R&D intensity targets and the fact that R&D explains relatively little of a country's innovation have not been enough to bring down the popularity of the R&D intensity indicator and its use as a policy flagship to foster innovation, competitiveness and economic growth (Carvalho 2018, p. 384).

Encouraging business R&D

While increasing government spending on R&D through research institutions and universities can be controlled through budget processes, incentivising R&D in the private sector is less controllable. Incentives to boost business expenditure on R&D can be highly effective at boosting national R&D levels and can assist industry to both modernise and develop new products. While outcomes from R&D expenditure at a firm level are not assured, R&D investment increases the likelihood of a firm patenting, although there is a more complex relationship with announcements of new products (Artz *et al.* 2010).

R&D tax credits seem to effectively incentivise firms to invest in R&D and innovate. R&D tax credits were shown to significantly improve innovation levels in the UK, particularly in enterprises that were financially constrained. The UK tax incentives boosted firm R&D by 10 per cent over a 5-year period (Dechezleprêtre *et al.* 2017; Guceri and Liu 2019). R&D tax credits were also found to have a significant and positive impact on patents and product innovation in New Zealand (Le and Jaffe 2017), while R&D subsidies improved innovation in firms, particularly smaller firms, in Italy (Bronzini and Piselli 2016).

Venture capital: effective, concentrated, intensely managed and growing

Venture capital (VC) as a source of funding for startups and scale-ups increased 5-fold between 2010–2019, but it is still tiny in volume compared to other forms of innovation finance such as R&D. VC investors contributed over $250 billion globally to startups in 2019 (Nanda 2020), compared to US$2.3 trillion in R&D funding (Heney 2020). The main difference between VC and R&D funding is that VC targets commercial innovation in the private sector, but to only a very small fraction of new business ventures.

In the US, which attracts the largest share of global VC, only around a 0.17 per cent of new businesses gain VC funding (Cornelius 2020). Funding is also highly concentrated both geographically and in the industries it targets. In 2020, just 11 cities accounted for over 60 per cent of global VC investments (Fig. 5.5) (Lerner 2020).

The geographic concentration of VC funds highlights the active role VC fund managers have in steering the development of young companies – often insisting on personal contact, nearby headquarters or that the personnel of portfolio companies attend training or events.

Famously, VC fund managers in Silicon Valley in the 1990s had a '20 min' rule: they wouldn't invest in companies that didn't have headquarters within a 20-minute drive from their office. There is evidence that this clustering and intense oversight paid off. Bernstein *et al.* (2016) found that reductions in travel times between a VC investor and a portfolio company were associated with increased patents and improved the likelihood of an eventual IPO or acquisition (Bernstein *et al.* 2016). VC funds also often work together to share the risk of a new venture, bringing in or consulting with each other to maximise the potential of a new venture succeeding. It appears that the mentoring, networks and management of new enterprises by

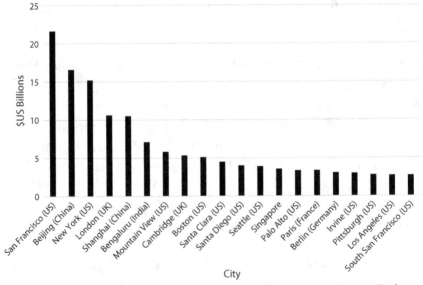

Fig. 5.5. Venture capital in technology companies by city, 2020. Source: Tech Nation Dealroom 2021 (Tech Nation 2021).

experienced VC managers contributes to the success of VC startups as much as the capital injection (Lerner 2020).

The bulk of VC is invested in ICT software and services, and financial, consumer and business services (Nanda 2020), although 2020 saw a spike in investment in the 'life sciences' areas, vaccines in particular (Pitchbook and National Venture Capital Association 2021). Many of these investments have been in 'winner-takes-all' business models – often networked digital platform companies that can form monopolistic markets by being the dominant provider or aggregator of services. There is also a trend towards larger deals in later-stage company development, moving away from the provision of seed or startup funding (Pitchbook and National Venture Capital Association 2021). The move towards bigger deals in more established businesses shows a growing risk aversion in the VC market, with investors seeking surer bets with potentially larger returns.

Despite the comparatively small amount of funding compared to R&D, VC funds pack a punch in stimulating innovation. Increases in VC funding are associated with significantly higher patenting rates. For instance, Kortum and Lerner (2000) found that venture capital accounted for 8 per cent of all US industrial innovation over the period of 1983–1992, despite being just 3 per cent of available R&D funds (Kortum and Lerner 2000). VC funds studied by Lerner and Kortum were three times more effective at stimulating patenting than corporate R&D expenditure. The authors also pointed out that: 'Both venture funding and patenting could be positively related to a third unobserved factor, the arrival of technological opportunities.'

Government-leveraged VC funds

Some governments have either created their own VC funds or provided matched funding for other investors in an attempt to attract more VC to a local startup ecosystem. They may also facilitate VC pitches, events and mentoring programs that provide the skills necessary for young companies to be 'pitch-ready'.

Government employees are often uncomfortable in the role of VC managers, as it interferes with market processes, can create conflicts of interest, and asks them to 'pick winners'. They are also unable to provide the market knowledge necessary to oversee the development of new companies. Government-funded VC may also crowd out commercial VC, overheat investment in certain sectors at critical times, attract criticism for funding companies for political purposes, or fund underperforming firms that compete with other firms in the marketplace. Lerner (2020) suggests that if governments do establish VC funds to stimulate innovation, they need to: (a) be administered by an independent body that can make purely commercial decisions away from political processes, and (b) insist on matching funds from industry, as industry can provide the intense oversight needed to make the investment work. In this way, government-backed VC can assist the existing VC industry by de-risking some of the bolder investments in seed or early-stage enterprises.

Sovereign wealth funds

Sovereign wealth funds (SWFs) have been growing rapidly since the early 2000s (Fig. 5.6). Nations have established SWFs as financial reserves in anticipation of future events such as an aging population,

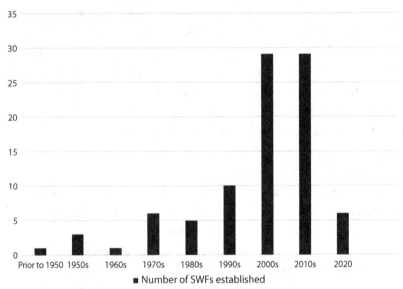

Fig. 5.6. Growth of sovereign wealth funds over the last 70 years. Source: Center for Governance of Change, IE University.

natural disasters, a decarbonised global economy and the need to invest in industrial change, or a drop in traditional values stores such as gold and precious metals.

Some of the largest sovereign wealth funds have been created from the proceeds of natural resource revenues, particularly the proceeds from the extraction of fossil fuels. These include Norway's Government Pension Fund Global (estimated to be worth around $1.3 trillion in 2020), Abu Dhabi Investment Authority ($650 billion in 2020), Kuwait Investment Authority ($535 billion) and Saudi Arabia's Public Investment Fund ($400 billion). Other countries have invested pension savings, infrastructure funds and disaster reserves. Combined, global SWFs had an estimated $9 trillion in assets under management in 2020 (Capape 2020).

The COVID-19 pandemic saw governments around the world go into unprecedented debt to provide fiscal support to their locked-down economies. In many cases, governments cashed in some of their assets held in SWFs to directly assist in budget spending. Certain SWFs were also called upon to invest in and support vaccination development efforts, the manufacture, procurement and distribution of medical supplies, and assist the healthcare sector in funding COVID treatment and infection control (Gupta *et al.* 2020).

More generally, though, SWFs are becoming more active in both funding innovative ventures and economic transition. The proportion of deals by SWFs in 'disruptive sectors' has been increasing. In 2018–19, biotech, software, fintech and data made up 47 per cent of all investment deals done by SWFs. Most of the funds for these deals have ended up in the US (31 per cent) and China (18 per cent), although smaller economies such as the Netherlands, Switzerland and Australia also received significant deals (Schena and Capape 2019).

Increasingly SWFs are investing in VC, despite the risks of investing in early-stage commercialisation. The lure of investing in the next Facebook, Apple or Google is great and, in some cases, SWFs have been put to work in creating new industries within domestic economies – hoping to provide employment through innovation investment:

One may question the rationale behind this interest of SWFs on technology. Indeed, SWFs have pursued VC investments for a variety of reasons, that can be summarized in three main motivations:

- Strong returns from innovative technologies (disrupting incumbents)
- Asset class diversification
- Diversification of local economies and other positive economic spill-overs (Rose and Capape 2019).

SWFs can also offer the VC market some attractive benefits. In particular, they can offer 'patient capital' or longer horizons before requesting liquidity than can traditional VC investors. They can use those longer time frames to create 'evergreen' funding, perpetual funding from the incomes of an initial endowment or investment. This can provide support for long-term projects or research – particularly useful for universities, basic research projects or infrastructure investments (Engel *et al.* 2020). There are also early signs that SWFs are becoming instrumental in the transition to a global low-carbon economy. Norway's large SWF recently announced it would divest in oil and gas exploration and invest instead in North Sea wind farms (Davies 2019; AFP 2021). But the political influences on the direction of this innovation funding, which promote economic and energy transformation, can also work against certain SWF investments. For instance, investments by the Chinese and Saudi SWFs are gaining more scrutiny, particularly in the US, as diplomatic tensions rise (Engel *et al.* 2020).

Unlocking innovation finance through regulation reforms

Finance for innovation can be unlocked through regulatory change. Two historic examples of regulatory changes that resulted in increased available funding for innovation include:

Prudent Man Rule: In 1979, changes to the US Employee Retirement Income Security Act of the Prudent Man Rule allowed institutional investors, and particularly pension funds, to invest up to 10 per cent of their funds into VC. This act changed what was considered to be 'prudent risk' for fund managers, who were previously prevented from investing pensions in VC due to their high-risk status. This significantly increased investment in VC funds in the US overnight:

> [T]he U.S. VC industry came into its own only after a regulatory change in 1979 that allowed pension funds to invest in VC. That rule change, known as the Prudent Man Rule, led to a greater than tenfold increase in the money entrusted to VC funds: VC funds raised $4.5 billion annually from 1982 to 1987, up from just $0.1 billion 10 years earlier (Strebulaev 2015).

Bayh–Dole Act: The Bayh–Dole Act enacted in the US in 1980 gave permission for a university, small business or not-for-profit enterprise to retain the patents or IP rights generated out of work enabled by federally funded grants. The purpose of this Act was to commercialise a far greater proportion of research funded by the federal government. This regulatory change produced an innovation shock across R&D-intensive research centres in the US, and an explosion in patenting by universities (Levenson 2005). Along with the patents came increases in funding allocated to commercialisation:

> Bayh–Dole has enabled a remarkable expansion of technology commercialization over the past few decades... Before 1980, fewer than 250 patents were issued to U.S. universities annually; discoveries were rarely commercialized for the public's benefit. By contrast, according to a recent survey by the Association of University Technology Managers (AUTM), in 2015 alone, U.S. universities garnered 6,164 U.S. patents, led to the formation of 950 new start-up companies, and generated more than 700 new commercial products (Association of American Universities and Association of Public & Land Grant Universities 2013).

These two regulatory changes in the US helped boost the VC industry in the early 1980s, increasing the funds available and the innovation to invest in, and have been cited as instrumental in the transition of Silicon Valley from a cluster of defence contractors to a cluster of ICT goods and services primarily for the business and consumer markets (Adams *et al.* 2018).

Table 5.1. Advantages and disadvantages of finance-led innovation efforts

Advantages	Disadvantages
• Venture capital (VC) backed companies have become some of the fastest growing disruptive companies in the world. Apple, Google, Facebook and Microsoft all started with VC funding, and arguably would not have developed without it. • Financing by sovereign wealth funds is growing around the world. These funds are keen to invest, and that investment is increasingly being channelled into both innovative or transformative businesses and projects and VC funds. • VC funds can import more than just the capital; they can import managerial expertise in commercialisation and production. • Tax credits can effectively incentivise R&D in the business sector and are particularly enabling for small or cash-constrained businesses with innovative ideas.	• There is no direct relationship between R&D and either innovation or economic growth. R&D is effective at promoting innovation and economic growth in large-market, advanced economies, and in high growth industries, although there are diminishing returns on that investment. • VC has been highly concentrated in both geographic areas, and in the industries it funds. This may be because fund managers need intense and face-to-face oversight of the funds in their portfolios. Establishing a VC industry outside the historic centres is difficult. • VC funds may be becoming more risk adverse, as they have trended towards supporting later-stage company growth in larger deals. • If not managed independently or prudently, government-backed VC funds can be wasteful spenders, or crowd out other investors looking to buy into innovative early-stage businesses.

Successful R&D and finance-led innovation: Israel and Silicon Wadi

In terms of economic development, Israel has several disadvantages: it is a small and relatively new nation of only 9 million people (2020), it sits on mainly desert lands with limited access to natural fresh water sources and few natural resources, and it has been involved in ongoing conflict with its Arab neighbours for decades. Despite these issues, over the last four decades Israel has become a global innovation powerhouse. In 2020, Israel ranked 13th on the Global Innovation Index and has one of the highest numbers of startups per capita. In the same year, Israel and the Tel-Aviv–Jerusalem cluster ranked 6th in the world on the Start-up Genome Ecosystem list, 4th on Blink's Startup Ecosystem Rankings and 23rd of the Global Innovation Index. The number of Israeli-born 'unicorn' companies (startup companies with a net value of over $1 billion) has been growing every year. In 2019, Israel could boast of 20 unicorns, and in 2020 that doubled to 40, and in 2021 this grew to 65 (Vidra 2020; techaviv 2021). In 2019, the export of ICT goods made up 10 per cent of all goods exported from Israel, with high technology goods contributing over 23 per cent of all manufactured exports (World Bank 2021b). Israel has also produced 10 Nobel Prize winners since 1990.

'Silicon Wadi' and 'Startup Nation' are the nicknames now given to the booming innovation ecosystem in Israel (de Fontenay and Carmel 2004; Senor and Singer 2009; Bordo 2018). Various authors have attributed the four-decade-long innovation boom in Israel to a multitude of factors, such as attractive regulation and ease of doing business, high immigration rates, good education and research institutions, an innovative military and high military spending, and good links to large consumer and tech markets in the US. Many Israeli-born companies list directly on the New York technology exchange (NASDAQ) and have headquarters in New York (Senor and Singer 2009). Other cited factors for its success include Israel's young population (with an average age of 24) and military conscription laws that create an alumni of young, talented, risk-taking and networked technologists trained directly in ICT fields such as data storage and cybersecurity (Shapiro 2013; Ferrari and Brack 2019). There is no doubt that all of these factors have played their part. The standout feature of the Israeli innovation boom, however, is the sheer level of financial investment (both public and private) in R&D and innovation.

Between 1999–2013 and 2015–2018, Israel had the highest R&D expenditure as a proportion of GDP in the world. In 2020, Israel's R&D expenditure is close to 5 per cent of its GDP, more than double the OECD average of 2.4 per cent (Fig. 5.7). Israel also attracts high levels of venture capital, second only to Singapore as a proportion of GDP (Cornell University *et al.* 2020; World Bank 2020).

The high investment in R&D and venture capital began in the late 1960s. Between 1969 and 1987, Israeli R&D expenditures rose by 14 per cent per year, and these expenditures were rewarded by a rapid increase in high-tech exports (Trajtenberg 2000). R&D funding administered by the Israeli Office of the Chief Scientist focused on high-tech companies and academic–industry consortia to build 'generic precompetitive technologies'. Technology incubators to nurture startups by assisting them to expand into export markets and gain venture capital funding. The focus on digital technology was deliberate, as it was seen as scalable and immediately exportable. The Office of the Chief Scientist, which allocates the funding, is an independent authority at arms-length from political processes.

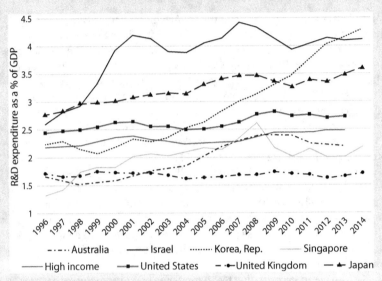

Fig. 5.7.   Research and development expenditure (% of GDP) for Israel and selected countries with available data. Source: World Bank.

The first private venture capital fund in Israel was Athena Venture Partners, founded in 1984 by ex-military personnel who saw an opportunity to launch Israeli innovation directly into the US market, rather than focus on the small domestic market. Nearly a decade later, in 1993, the Israeli government established Yozma, which attracted foreign venture capital with state funding and directed that funding into local startups. Yozma is now considered the gold standard in how governments should structure their finance-led innovation efforts in regard to attracting foreign venture capital. Unlike many other government-backed, early-stage venture funds, Yozma requests matching funds from industry and shares the risk in investing in early industrial innovation. Yozma's architects also saw the importation of foreign expertise, market knowledge and networks as being as valuable as the funding itself:

> *Intriguingly the key goal of this effort [to establish Yozma] was the desire to bring in foreign venture capitalists' investment expertise and network of contacts to Israel. The need for this assistance was highlighted by the failure of the nation's early efforts to promote high-technology entrepreneurship. One assessment concluded that fully 60% of entrepreneurs in prior programs had been successful in meeting their technical goals but nonetheless failed because the entrepreneurs were unable to market their products or raise capital for further development (Lerner 2020).*

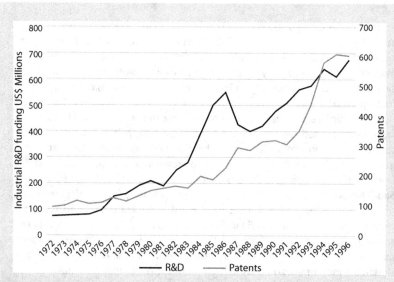

Fig. 5.8. R&D funding in Israel and number of Israeli registered patents 1972–1996
Source: Graph recreated from Trajtenberg (2000).

In an early review of the impact of R&D funding in Israel, Trajtenberg (2000) plotted the rise of R&D funding against increases in patents and saw a lagged correlation between R&D funding and patent numbers (Fig. 5.8). In terms of patents per capita, Israel performed above competitive and comparable countries such as Finland, Taiwan and South Korea over this period.

There is no doubt that focusing on high levels of finance – both R&D and venture capital – has fuelled Israel's innovation and economic trajectory over the last 40 years. The development of a trained technology and finance-savvy network of entrepreneurs has now allowed Israel to become one of the few successful 'Silicon-somethings' to emerge.

Less successful R&D and finance-led innovation effort: The Kingdom of Saudi Arabia

A Middle Eastern neighbour of Israel, the Kingdom of Saudi Arabia (Saudi Arabia) is a religious, non-democratic, socially conservative and oil-rich nation of 33 million people. In 2019, fuel exports accounted for over 80 per cent of all merchandise exports from Saudi Arabia compared to the global average of around 13 per cent (World Bank 2021a). In 1971, Saudi Arabia created a sovereign wealth fund (the Saudi Public Investment Fund) to invest some of the profits of oil exports into innovation and infrastructure of vital projects associated with the country's major industries: oil refining and extraction, petrochemicals and electricity. In 2015, however, the *Saudi Vision 2030*, a foresight report that created 'an ambitious yet achievable blueprint' for the nation, outlined a pathway away from economic dependence on oil and into a far more diversified economy built on health, education, infrastructure and tourism. This report coincided with a global trend towards decarbonisation and, in particular, the rise of electric vehicles and renewable energy. Investment from the Public Investment Fund is critical in developing this new vision for Saudi Arabia and transitioning the Saudi economy away from its dependence on oil revenues (Saudi Public Investment Fund 2021). With estimated assets of close to $400 billion, the Saudi Public Investment Fund is now one of the largest sovereign wealth funds in the world. It aims to have $2 trillion in assets under management by 2030 (US Saudi Business Council 2021), and has been making significant investments globally in highly innovative companies including Boeing, Disney and Facebook.

The primary focus of many sovereign wealth funds is not necessarily to stimulate domestic innovation, but to invest wisely on the global stock market and to maintain or grow its value. For example, a similar sovereign wealth fund established by Norway in 1990 to invest the proceeds of the North Sea oil and gas revenues only invested in global bonds, equities and real estate up until recently. Incredibly, Norway's sovereign wealth fund, estimated to valued at around $1.3 trillion, owns a 1.4 per cent stake in all the world's publicly listed companies (Ghosh 2021). Like the Saudi Public Investment Fund, the Norwegian Fund did little to transition the local economy away from employment in the oil and gas sectors until recently. In 2015, a sudden drop in oil prices meant the Norwegian government had to dip into its ballooning sovereign wealth fund due to high domestic unemployment caused by the flagging oil and gas sector. This appears to have been the trigger to start using the funds to diversify the Norwegian economy more generally.

Although not the sole purpose of the fund, the existence of Saudi Arabia's large and well-established sovereign wealth fund has given Saudi Arabia a rare advantage in having the ability to re-invest in the creation of new industries in times of industrial and environmental shifts. Despite the Public Investment Fund, investment in R&D within Saudi Arabia remains extremely low, at under 1 per cent of GDP. By comparison, the global average for R&D expenditure in 2018 was 2.3 per cent of GDP, while the average for high income countries is 2.6 per cent of GDP (Cornell University *et al.* 2020; World Bank 2020).

Venture capital attraction in Saudi Arabia, while rising, remains less than 0.1 per cent of GDP – one of the lowest of the world's higher income countries.

Saudi Arabia also lags behind in its expected development on the Global Innovation Index – ranked at 66th place (Cornell University *et al.* 2020) alongside middle-income countries such as Tunisia, Belarus, Iran and Colombia. The Start-up Genome report suggests that despite newer government incentives, median seed funding and software engineer wages in the country's capital, Riyadh, are well below global averages. News reports also tell of drastic industry shortages in coding and software engineers (Tashkandi 2020). Patents awarded to Saudi-based companies have been rising, however, with the Saudi oil company, Saudi Aramco, being awarded a significant proportion of new patents for petrochemical/refining advances (World Bank 2021c).

In its efforts to help Saudi Arabia fulfil its *2030 Vision* of a far more diversified economy, the Public Investment Fund has stated that its key investment objectives in 2021–2025 will be in aerospace, automotive industries, transport and logistics, food and agriculture and construction and building. It will also invest over $40 billion in the domestic market annually, with a target of a 21 per cent share of assets in new and growth sectors (Madslien 2016). Interestingly, it plans to localise 'cutting edge technology and knowledge through the Public Investment Fund' (Fig. 5.9). In 2019, the Public Investment Fund created a new venture capital fund, Jada, to invest over US$1.07 billion in local startups and

Fig. 5.9. Saudi and US researchers study and test solar energy production and storage in Denver, Colorado. Public domain image by USA Department of Energy from United States.

SMEs (Jada 2020; Paracha 2020). While it may be too early to see the impacts of the *2030 Vision* and change in strategic investment decisions within Saudi Arabia, it would seem as though the primary effort of the Public Investment Fund is to make strategic and profitable investments in innovative, high-growth companies grown elsewhere. This would counteract the loss of national income from oil in the wake of global carbon emission regulation, while slowly growing domestic industries in new sectors to maintain employment levels. The *2030 Vision* also makes it clear that Saudi Arabia values retaining its social traditions and religious observance while modernising industry. The first pillar of the new vision is to retain Saudi Arabia's status as 'the heart of the Arab and Islamic worlds' through its custodianship of two of the most holy sites in Islam; the second pillar is to become a global investment powerhouse, while the third and last pillar is to transform the domestic economy.

Summary

The relationship between available finance and innovation metrics is not clear cut. Different forms of finance have different outcomes: R&D spending is vital to funding higher education research, but its efficiency is dependent on the translation of research outcomes to industry. R&D spending by industry itself is associated with innovative businesses, but it has different effects in different sectors. Total R&D spending at a national level increases innovation levels in higher-income, large market countries, but technology adoption is more efficient in increasing innovation in lower-income or smaller-market countries. Venture capital has the most impact in new product development and new company creation but it is highly concentrated in its geographic reach and target sectors. Its success in creating innovation outcomes may be due to the strict management of portfolio companies by VC fund managers and investors. Rapidly growing investments in sovereign wealth funds may provide a new source of innovation investment, particularly in times where rapid industry transition is needed.

References

Adams SB, Chambers D, Schultz M (2018) A moving target: the geographic evolution of Silicon Valley, 1953–1990. *Business History* **60**, 859–883. doi:10.1080/00076791.2017.1346612

AFP (2021) Norway sovereign wealth fund buys first renewable energy stake. *The Economic Times*, 8 April. Film City, Noida. <https://energy.economictimes.indiatimes.com/news/renewable/norway-sovereign-wealth-fund-buys-first-renewable-energy-stake/81961002>

Artz KW, Norman PM, Hatfield DE, Cardinal LB (2010) A longitudinal study of the impact of R&D, patents, and product innovation on firm performance. *Journal of Product Innovation Management* **27**, 725–740. doi:10.1111/j.1540-5885.2010.00747.x

Association of American Universities, Association of Public & Land Grant Universities (2013) *University Technology Commercialisation, Federal Research Funding, the Bayh-Dole Act and Federal Support for Entrepreneurship/Gap Funding Programs.* Association of Public & Land Grant Universities, Washington DC.

Bernstein S, Giroud X, Townsend RR (2016) The impact of venture capital monitoring. *The Journal of Finance* **71**, 1591–1622. doi:10.1111/jofi.12370

Bordo M (2018) Israeli tech's identity crisis: startup nation or scale up nation? *Forbes* 14 May. Forbes, Jersey City, NJ. <https://www.forbes.com/sites/startupnationcentral/2018/05/14/israeli-techs-identity-crisis-startup-nation-or-scale-up-nation/?sh=274ea6dcef48>

Bronzini R, Piselli P (2016) The impact of R&D subsidies on firm innovation. *Research Policy* **45**, 442–457. doi:10.1016/j.respol.2015.10.008

Capape J (2020) Executive Summary and preface. In *Sovereign Wealth Funds 2020: Fighting the pandemic, embracing change.* (Ed. J Capape) pp. 5–11. Center for Governance of Change: IE University, Madrid.

Carvalho A (2018) Wishful thinking about R&D policy targets: what governments promise and what they actually deliver. *Science & Public Policy* **45**, 373–391. doi:10.1093/scipol/scx069

Cornelius P (2020) Sources of funding innovation and entrepreneurship. In *Global Innovation Index 2020.* (Eds S Dutta, B Lanvin, S Wunsch-Vincent) pp. 77–86. Cornell University, INSEAD, WIPO, Ithaca, Fontainebleau, and Geneva.

Cornell University, INSEAD, WIPO (2020) Key findings. In *The Global Innovation Index 2020: Who will finance innovation?.* (Eds S Dutta, B Lanvin, S Wunsch-Vincent) pp. xvi–xxix. Cornell University, INSEAD, WIPO, Ithaca, Fountainebleau, Geneva.

Davies R (2019) Norway's $1tn wealth fund to divest from oil and gas exploration. *The Guardian*, London, 8 May.

de Fontenay C, Carmel E (2004) Israel's Silicon Wadi. In *Building High-Tech Clusters: Silicon Valley and Beyond.* (Eds T Bresnahan, A Gambardella) pp. 40–77. Cambridge University Press, Cambridge, UK.

Dechezleprêtre A, Einiö E, Martin R, Nguyen K-T, Van Reenen J (2017) Do tax incentives for research increase firm innovation? An RD design for R&D. MIT Economics, Cambridge, Massachusetts. <http://economics.mit.edu/files/12817>

Ejermo O, Kander A, Svensson Henning M (2011) The R&D-growth paradox arises in fast-growing sectors. *Research Policy* **40**, 664–672. doi:10.1016/j.respol.2011.03.004

Engel J, Barbary V, Hamirani H, Saklatvala K (2020) Sovereign wealth funds and innovation investing in an era of mounting uncertainty. In *Global Innovation Index 2020: Who will finance innovation?* (Eds S Dutta, B Lanvin, S Wunsch-Vincent) pp. 89–102. Cornell University, INSEAD, WIPO, Ithaca, Fontainebleau, Geneva.

Ferrari J, Brack A (2019) *From Israel's 'start-up nation', 4 lessons in innovation.* World Economic Forum, Cologny, Switzerland.

Ghosh P (2021) Norway's sovereign wealth fund makes first investment in renewable energy infrastructure. *Forbes*, 7 April. Forbes, Jersey City NJ. <https://www.forbes.com/sites/palashghosh/2021/04/07/norways-sovereign-wealth-fund-makes-first-investment-in-renewable-energy-infrastructure/?sh=33ce694d3f6d>

Guceri I, Liu L (2019) Effectiveness of fiscal incentives for R&D: quasi-experimental evidence. *American Economic Journal: Economic Policy* **11**, 266–291. doi:10.1257/pol.20170403

Gupta G, Menzemer M, Schena P (2020) A year of 'living dangerously' – the COVID pandemic and sovereign wealth fund direct investments in 2019–2020. In *Sovereign Wealth Funds 2020.* (Ed. J Papape.) pp. 12–20. Center for Governance of Change: IE University, Madrid.

Heney P (2020) Global R&D investments unabated in spending growth. *R&D World* 19 March. WTWH Media LLC, Cleveland. <https://www.rdworldonline.com/global-rd-investments-unabated-in-spending-growth/>

Howitt P, Aghion P (1998) Capital accumulation and innovation as complementary factors in long-run growth. *Journal of Economic Growth* **3**, 111–130. doi:10.1023/A:1009769717601

Jada (2020) *General overview and vision.* Jada, Riyadh <http://jada.com.sa/EN/home.html>

Kortum S, Lerner J (2000) Assessing the contribution of venture capital to innovation. *The RAND Journal of Economics* **31**, 674–692. doi:10.2307/2696354

Le T, Jaffe AB (2017) The impact of R&D subsidy on innovation: evidence from New Zealand firms. *Economics of Innovation and New Technology* **26**, 429–452. doi:10.1080/10438599.2016.1213504

Lerner J (2020) Government incentives for entrepreneurship. In *Global Innovation Index 2020: Who will finance innovation?* (Eds S Dutta, B Lanvin, S Wunsch-Vincent) pp. 105–112. Cornell University, INSEAD, and WIPO, Ithaca, Fontainebleau, and Geneva.

Levenson D (2005) Consequences of the Bayh-Dole Act. 6.901 Final Paper. MIT, Massachusetts, 12 December. <https://ocw.mit.edu/courses/electrical-engineering-and-computer-science/6-901-inventions-and-patents-fall-2005/projects/bayh_dole.pdf>.

Liu W-H (2016) Intellectual property rights, FDI, R&D and economic growth: a cross-country empirical analysis. *World Economy* **39**, 983–1004. doi:10.1111/twec.12304

Madslien J (2016) Norway seeks to diversify its economy as oil earnings plunge. BBC, London, 10 February. <https://www.bbc.com/news/business-35318236>

Nanda R (2020) Financing 'tough tech' innovation. In *Global Innovation Index 2020; Who will finance innovation?* (Eds S Dutta, B Lanvin, S Wunsch-Vincent) pp. 113–119. Cornell University, INSEAD, WIPO, Ithaca, Fontainebleau, Geneva.

Paracha ZN (2020) Saudi's public investment fund launches Jada, a $1.07 billion fund of funds to invest in startups and SMEs. Menabytes, Lahore, Pakistan, 18 December. <https://www.menabytes.com/pif-jada/>

Pessoa A (2010) R&D and economic growth: how strong is the link? *Economics Letters* **107**, 152–154. doi:10.1016/j.econlet.2010.01.010

Pitchbook and National Venture Capital Association (2021) Venture Monitor Q1 2021. National Venture Capital Association, Washington DC and San Francisco. <https://nvca.org/wp-content/uploads/2021/04/Q1_2021_PitchBook_Venture_Monitor.pdf>

Romer PM (1990) Endogenous technological change. *Journal of Political Economy* **98**, S71–S102. doi:10.1086/261725

Rose P, Capape J (2019) Technology, venture capital and SWFs: The role of the government forging innovation and change. In *Sovereign Wealth Fund 2019: managing continuity, embracing change.* (Ed. J Capape.) pp. 23–26. Center for the Governance of Change, IE University, Madrid.

Saudi Public Investment Fund (2021) Public Investment Fund Program 2021–2025. PIF, Riyadh. <https://www.pif.gov.sa/VRP%202025%20Downloadables%20EN/PIFStrategy2021-2025-EN.pdf>

Schena P, Capape J (2019) Managing continuity, embracing change: sovereign wealth fund direct investments 2018–2019. In *Sovereign Wealth Funds.* (Ed. J Capape.) pp. 23–36. Center for Governance of Change; IE University, Madrid.

Senor D, Singer P (2009) *Start-up Nation: The story of Israel's Economic Miracle.* Twelve Books, New York.

Shapiro G (2013) What are the secrets behind Israel's growing innovative edge? *Forbes*, 7 November.

Srinivasan R (2021) *Platform Business Models: Frameworks, concepts and design.* Springer Singapore, Singapore.

Strebulaev IA (2015) How much does venture capital drive the US economy? Insights by Stanford Business. Graduate School of Stanford Business, Stanford, 21 October. <https://www.gsb.stanford.edu/insights/how-much-does-venture-capital-drive-us-economy>

Sylwester K (2001) R&D and economic growth. *Knowledge, Technology & Policy* **13**, 71–84. doi:10.1007/BF02693991

Tashkandi H (2020) Coding 101: why Saudis should learn to talk to their computers. *Arab News*.23 August. < https://www.arabnews.com/node/1723181/saudi-arabia>

Tech Nation (2021) *The future UK tech built: Tech Nation Report 2021.* Tech Nation, London. <https://technation.io/report2021/>

techaviv (2021) *Iraeli founded unicorns.* techaviv, Tel Aviv, 12 November. <https://www.techaviv.com/unicorns>

Trajtenberg M (2000) *R&D Policy in Israel: An overview and reassessment.* Samuel Neaman Institute for Advanced Science and Technology; Technion – Israel Institute of Technology, Tel Aviv.

Ulku H (2004) *R & D, Innovation, and Economic Growth: An empirical analysis.* International Monetary Fund, Washington, DC.

Ulku H (2007) R&D, innovation, and growth: evidence from four manufacturing sectors in OECD countries. *Oxford Economic Papers* **59**, 513–535. doi:10.1093/oep/gpl022

US Saudi Business Council (2021) *Saudi Arabia's Public Investment Fund: New Strategies, Investments and Diversification.* US Saudi Business Council, Vienna US, Riyadh Kingdom of Saudi Arabia.

Vidra E (2020) The Israeli Unicorn Landscape. VC Café, London, 2 October. <https://www.vccafe.com/2020/10/02/the-israeli-unicorn-landscape/>

World Bank (2020) *Research and Development expenditure (% of GDP).* World Bank: Washington DC. <https://data.worldbank.org/indicator/GB.XPD.RSDV.GD.ZS>

World Bank (2021a) *Fuel exports (% of merchandise exports).* World Bank, Washington, DC. <https://data.worldbank.org/indicator/TX.VAL.FUEL.ZS.UN>

World Bank (2021b) *High tech exports.* World Bank:Washington DC. <https://data.worldbank.org/indicator/TX.VAL.TECH.CD>

World Bank (2021c) *Patent applications, residents.* World Bank: Washington DC. <https://data.worldbank.org/indicator/IP.PAT.RESD >

Zachariadis M (2003) RD, innovation, and technological progress: a test of the Schumpeterian framework without scale effects. *The Canadian Journal of Economics. Revue Canadienne d'Economique* **36**, 566–586. doi:10.1111/1540-5982.t01-2-00003

6

Technology-led innovation

Aim

To modernise government services through the application of new and emerging technologies

Technology-led innovation has a sharp focus on applying and developing new or emerging technologies using public sector procurement. It could also be called procurement-led innovation, although the emphasis is slightly different. Technology-led innovation examines new and emerging technologies (e.g. radio, drones or blockchain) and looks for applications in government services. The intellectual property (IP) remains in the private sector to be commercialised, and so contributes to building the local industry. Procurement-led innovation, on the other hand, allocates a proportion of public sector procurement budgets for innovative applications and explores a range of technologies to fill a public sector need – that is, it is needs-led. The OECD calls this Public Procurement for Innovation. There are subtle differences between technology-led and procurement-led innovation but in practice they go hand-in-hand and are almost indistinguishable.

> Governments are increasingly recognising the immense power of public procurement to solve global societal challenges, improve productivity and boost innovation, while ensuring value for money. Public procurement represents 12 percent of gross domestic product (GDP) and

29 percent of total government expenditures on average across OECD countries, a clear sign of its potential to support broader policy objectives, including the fostering of innovation (OECD 2017, p. 3).

In many cases, the benefits of a technological application are still theoretical when it first begins to be pitched to government bodies for use in public sector settings. Taking a technology-led approach is about exploring and developing the high-potential technologies, even before all the applications and benefits are known.

For technology-led innovation to occur, governments need to:

- be highly technologically innovative and open to experimentation
- dedicate funds for change, transformation or technological co-development
- have the expertise to be able to assess the benefits of new or emerging technology
- know how to pilot new technologies in low-risk environments before larger scale adoption
- have procurement mechanisms to adopt the technologies from inventors, startups and early-stage companies and scale them up quickly from a pilot.

Why governments tend not to be first movers in implementing new technologies

Governments are generally bureaucratic, siloed and risk-adverse with taxpayer funds. This is not a criticism; it is their job to be risk adverse and not wasteful. This has made innovation and technological development historically difficult in many areas of government. A large reform project will also often need political support from the Minister in charge.

Areas of government that have been the most innovative are those with greater technological freedom, skills in project management – particularly in technology implementation – and those that have less budgetary oversight. Typically, these have been defence departments and certain areas within health, transport services or border security.

Defence departments are also often exempted from many procurement restrictions resulting from free-trade agreements, for instance, on the grounds of national security.

In many cases, public servants and heads of departments can see the potential of new technologies to contribute to service efficiencies, but don't have the funds or the power to be able to commit to technological experimentation, customisation or implementation. Instead, they are expected to procure tried and tested 'off-the-shelf' products and proven technologies. It is often more important for the public sector to spend safely than to become technological leaders in their field or support expensive technological co-development.

Most government departments do not have internal research and development (R&D) units. Instead, R&D is outsourced to the private sector or research institutions, and the modernisation of government services is often left to the expertise and competencies of the departmental leaders and project managers.

There is no incentive within the public sector to gain first-mover status in the adoption or development of new technologies, except perhaps where there are great cost efficiencies to be made. Public sector procurement rules also often exclude buying from companies that are less than 5 years old when a contract is over a certain amount. This means local industry and the startup sector are often deprived of the public sector market when developing or commercialising new technologies.

If governments remain second-movers in the adoption of technology government, they miss the chance to support the development of new local industries or industry transition through the government marketplace and procurement.

Teaching government how to play with new technologies

To overcome some of the risks of implementing new systems or technologies, some governments or government bodies have established public service innovation laboratories. Examples include the OECD's Observatory of Public Sector Innovation, Denmark's Disruption Taskforce, Singapore's Public Service Division Innovation Laboratory, and the UK's National Endowment for Science, Technology and the Arts (NESTA). Regulatory sandboxes and experimental platforms are also increasing in popularity. In Australia, the Energy Market Commission and Australian Securities and Investments Commission (ASIC) have established regulatory sandboxes for energy-tech and fintech development, including blockchain, mobile applications and use of platforms. These allow regulatory exemptions for proof-of-concept trials and technological development for both public and private sector settings.

Places of invention

In 2014, the Smithsonian National Museum of American History showcased six US hotspots of invention from the last 200 years (Lemelson Center for the Study of Invention and Innovation 2014; Molella and Karvellas 2015; Cameron *et al.* unpublished). The research from the exhibitions showed that US government procurement and internal R&D played an instrumental role in the initiation of four out of the six hotspots chosen: Silicon Valley in California, Medical Alley in Minnesota, Hartford in Connecticut, and Fort Collins in Colorado. The role of government in the development of those four hotspots was primarily that of lead customer and procurer of goods and services. R&D contracts and education institutions also featured, but it was government contracts that powered much of the work behind the innovation clusters. Governments contracted for the technological benefits – not to build the cluster, *per se.* The clustering and building of industry was almost a by-product.

Breakthrough inventions at the start of the development of these innovative clusters usually came from a pressing public service need, such as winning a war, providing cardiac health services, or transitioning an energy sector. The early innovations included assembly-line production and precision engineering, integrated circuits (the first computer chips), externally worn pacemakers and green-energy systems. These technologies were then backed by large government contracts or support in public sector settings. This provided the initial support needed to build successful companies that commercialised the product

Fig. 6.1. Steps for technology-led innovation.

beyond the initial application and, importantly, often supported early-stage companies and startups through the first 5 years of their existence – the 'valley of death' (see Fig. 6.1 and Chapter 5).

Government procurement can build powerful industry clusters – SBIR

The development of industry clusters through internal efforts to modernise public service delivery is not the standard or obvious route of innovation policy, or in building innovative clusters. For this reason, it is often neglected as formal innovation policy, although there are mechanisms available in some countries to support innovation through government procurement. The US and the UK, for instance, have developed small business innovation and research (SBIR) funding, which commits and quarantines departmental funds to procuring innovative technologies from small and early-stage companies.

US government requires 11 of its agencies with an R&D budget of over $100 million to commit 3.2 per cent of their R&D budget to the SBIR funds. The stated aims of the program are to:

- stimulate technological innovation
- meet federal research and development needs

- foster and encourage participation in innovation and entrepreneurship by women and socially or economically disadvantaged persons
- increase private-sector commercialisation of innovations derived from federal research and development funding (Small Business Innovation Research 2020).

The funds committed to support startups and innovators through SBIR funding are not insubstantial. Overall, the US federal government commits over \$2.2 billion annually to the SBIR and its related fund, the Small Business Technology Transfer (STTR) program (2020).

The returns on investment for SBIR funds have been large, although they vary dramatically from agency to agency. For every SBIR dollar invested through the US Air Force SBIR/STTR fund, \$4.10 is contributed back to the US economy (Subcommittee on Technology and Innovation 2009; US Air Force 2019; Small Business Innovation Research 2020).

> Our commercialization efforts have served to bridge the 'valley of death' between SBIR/STTR companies and the larger acquisition community. Our operational experimentation and technology demonstrations have linked small businesses with their customers and given companies unparalleled insight into the needs of the warfighter. Our AFWERX 'Front Door' has simplified the entry point into the SBIR/STTR program and streamlined the process of doing business with the Air Force (Shahady 2019).

The problems with technology-based innovation efforts: wasteful, experimental and open to criticism

The main problem with technology-led innovation is that it is risky and costly to invest in technology development. When things go wrong, governments often suffer adverse media exposure and are labelled incompetent. Industry development is not seen as the function of government procurement in most jurisdictions, and investing too early in technologies for public services can lead to wasteful spending, stranded assets or great public inconvenience (although 'inconvenience' may be a euphemism for the damaged lives or livelihoods that may result from badly managed government systems reform).

There is often a dearth of good technology project managers in government; people who can adequately assess the risks of new technology and are skilled at staged implementation and testing. Examples of large and costly IT project failures can be found in almost every jurisdiction. These haunt government decision-makers, making them timid to try large reforms that rely too heavily on experimental technology and modernising technological systems. Notable examples of technological reforms that have failed include:

- **The UK government's failed national electronic health record system**. The National Program for IT (NPfIT) was launched in 2002 and sought to introduce an integrated patient records system across the UK's National Health Service. NPfIT cost over $9.8 billion to build but delivered just 2 per cent of promised benefits. In addition, it created broad resistance in the user population of doctors and health professionals and was eventually dismantled in 2011 (Justinia 2017).
- **The US Government's Secure Border Initiative Network (SBInet) project**. SBInet was meant to create a virtual barrier between the US and Mexico along a 53-mile (85 km) section of the border. In 2006, Boeing was contracted by the US Department of Homeland Security (DHS) to develop an innovative system of radar, video and electronic records to improve detection, prevent illegal entry, and efficiently identify and judiciously process people who did illegally cross into the US. After 2 years of development, the project was cancelled before becoming operational. The partial development cost over $1 billion (Homeland Security News Wire 2010).
- **The Queensland Government's Health Payroll Upgrade**. The Health Department in Queensland, Australia, upgraded its aging and outdated payroll system in 2008 with a $6.19 million contract to IBM. The project lasted 3 years longer than

anticipated and eventually went live only to leave thousands of doctors, nurses and other health workers over- or under-paid for months. The payroll mistakes eventually cost the state's taxpayers an estimated A$1.25 billion to correct, led to sustained industrial action and caused the Health Minister to resign. There was also a change of government at the following election. (Willis 2015; Charette 2019).

Most governments are elected for only a short period and many see the risks of large public service reform as too risky for their tenure.

Despite the risks of experimenting with new technology in public service settings, the rewards can be great. Without a doubt the largest and most successful technology clusters in the world have developed on the back of public service procurement contracts.

How technology-led innovation built Silicon Valley[1]

The West Coast of the US, including Silicon Valley, San Francisco Bay area and Seattle, has been the undisputed global leader of information and communications technology (ICT) innovation for over four decades. Over the past century, the West Coast has been the birthplace of global ICT companies such as Hewlett-Packard, Microsoft, Apple, Facebook, Google, Sun Microsystems, Oracle, CISCO, QualComm, Uber, Airbnb, Lyft and Amazon. The Los Angeles, Seattle, Silicon Valley and San Francisco Bay area attract over half of all venture capital in the US. This totalled over $85 billion in venture capital (VC) deals in 2020 (Pitchbook and NVCA 2020).

The companies founded in Silicon Valley and headquartered on the West Coast had a market capitalisation of over $9 trillion in 2021, up from just $2.7 trillion in 2018 (Candelon *et al.* 2018; Companies Market Cap 2021). This wealth brings enormous spillover effects in market and industry knowledge and startup assistance. As these companies also trade in data and market knowledge, the geographic concentration of these companies creates a technopole of information power that can wield enormous hegemonic advantage over other countries and regions.

But Silicon Valley and the West Coast of the US didn't always have this wealth, power or reputation. At beginning of the 20th century, the Santa Clara Valley – where Silicon Valley would eventually grow – was a quiet rural precinct of fruit orchards and small farm ventures. Most innovation in the US occurred on the East Coast where the great inventors such as Thomas Edison, Alexander Bell, George Westinghouse, Samuel Morse, Isaac Singer, Nikola Tesla and George Eastman resided. So why did Silicon Valley emerge on the West Coast? What factors created the world's largest cluster of ICT firms and innovation growth?

The clustering story for Silicon Valley started long before silicon was used in computing, and instead dates back to the beginning of the 20th century. In 1898, America acquired a range of new territories in the Pacific and the Caribbean when it won the Spanish–American War. These new territories incentivised the development of new naval bases on the West Coast of the US. There were constant issues with communications between the West Coast naval bases and naval facilities across the Pacific in the Philippines, Guam and the Marshall Islands, as well as those in the Caribbean; Puerto Rico and Cuba. Thankfully there was a promising new technology on the horizon that could solve that: radio.

In 1899, Italian inventor Guglielmo Marconi successfully demonstrated radio communication for the first time at the America's Cup yacht race in New Jersey. Key personnel of the US Navy were present and instantly became interested. Within 5 years, the US government had contracted Marconi's Wireless Telegraph Co. to build radio towers up and down both the east and west coasts of the US. An Australian-born Stanford graduate, Cyril Elwell, formed the Federal Telegraph Co. in Palo Alto (where Silicon Valley now sits) and created a new radio technology called the 'Paulson arc', a stronger electromagnetic signal than the competition at the time. Using this technology, the Federal Telegraph Co. created the world's first global-scale radio communications system in 1912 (Sturgeon 2000).

Dr Lee de Forest, an ex-employee of the Federal Telegraph Co., was also an early inventor and adopter of radio technology who gained naval contracts to build transmission towers. De Forest pioneered the use of vacuum tubes as detectors and amplifiers of radio waves. He pitched the technology to the Navy and then worked with naval personnel to co-develop the technology and make improvements to installations on land and ships.

The US Navy was very open to being pitched new technologies and ideas, and navy engineers often tested and wrote detailed appraisals of the new equipment developed in the laboratories of private inventors and companies. The Navy worked closely with the contractors to improve the designs for military use and were constantly seeking greater reliability, distance, clarity in reception, and signal amplification in radio technologies (Fig. 6.2).

Fig. 6.2. Testing the functionality of newly developed radio communications and training navy personnel in its use, Annapolis. *The Sunday Star* 1917, Washington DC. Image in the public domain, stored in archives at the Smithsonian National Museum of American History.

In many instances, naval personnel drove innovation by requesting functionality that had not yet been developed. A piece of personal correspondence in the Smithsonian National Museum of American History describes the actions of Admiral SC Hooper, one of the primary commissioning officers in the Navy's Bureau of Steam Engineering in 1899. His assistant wrote:

> 'You are modest', I replied, 'You do not mention that much of the perfection to which radio has attained today in its application to Naval use has been due to your work, to the many years during which you forced the issue and made Navy radio go ahead faster than it wanted to.' Manuscript – Loften Clark Hooper to Admiral Stanford C Hooper 1939.

Development in the electronics technology sector in the US increased during the Second World War, Korean War and subsequent Cold War periods. The Second World War saw the rapid growth in technologies companies around the San Francisco Bay area, particularly in the final stages, which saw the Pacific theatre focus military attention on defending the West Coast as well as the East.

By the time the US entered the Second World War in 1941, after the attack on Pearl Harbor by the Japanese Imperial Forces, it was apparent that the Germans and Japanese had far superior radio equipment. Banks of ground and mobile transmitters and receivers, and on-board aeroplane-installed radars, allowed the German and Japanese armies to identify and shoot down hundreds of Allied Forces planes and avoid being shot down when on their own bombing missions (Blank 2008).

For the first time, the US was fighting wars on both sides of the country: against the Germans across the Atlantic in the east and against the Japanese Imperial forces to the west in the Pacific. The Pacific territories were utilised by the US military for naval bases: Marshall Islands, Guam, Alaska, Northern Mariana Islands, US Virgin Islands, Hawaii and American Samoa, among others.

The US military sought to engage the country's best electronics engineers in a program known as ELINT (electronic intelligence) in a desperate effort to better detect enemy planes, avoid detection, create reliable communications and develop surveillance and radar systems that gave the Allied Forces a tactical advantage. At the time, the country's best engineers were mostly employed by universities, and two in particular – Harvard and MIT. They were quickly seconded into military research laboratories, such as the Harvard Radio Research Laboratory, all of which were located on the East Coast.

After the Second World War, a couple of key people moved to the San Francisco area and Stanford University. Dr Fred Terman from the Harvard Research Laboratory created a centre of excellence at Stanford University. Terman encouraged his students to commercialise their research and form companies rather than undertake higher degrees; helpfully, Terman had military and research connections on the East Coast. He fought hard to bring Federal funding and research contracts to Stanford and Stanford students. Notable students of Terman included William Hewlett and David Packard, who went on to form Hewlett-Packard, or HP, in 1939.

Just after the war, electronics engineer and eventual Nobel Prize winner William Shockley also moved back to the San Francisco area, in part to be near his elderly mother. He brought with him one of the 25 licences issued from Bell Laboratories for the production of semiconductors (which replaced vacuum tubes as switches in electronics and radio equipment). Shockley set up his laboratory in the Palo Alto area south of San Francisco, which became colloquially named 'Silicon Valley' when silicon replaced germanium as the material used in semiconductor switches.

With investment funding from New York millionaire Sherman Fairchild, a group of eight scientists split from Shockley's laboratory in the 1950s to form Fairchild Computers. The company started producing integrated circuits, a technology developed simultaneously by Robert Noyce of Fairchild Computers and Jack Kilby of Texas Instruments. The integrated circuit became the 'silicon chip' and Jack Kilby went on to win the Nobel Prize in Physics in 2000.

Integrated circuits were based on a new metal printing technique, but their application to a range of computing devices was not immediately obvious. Defence contracts for semiconductors and integrated circuits were critical in their further development. Large defence contracts provided the incentive to innovate the manufacturing process, which dramatically reduced the cost per unit and made them affordable for a range of new products, including non-military applications such as calculators and, eventually, personal computers.

The Cold War and the Korean and Vietnam wars were also all on the Pacific side of the US, and so the Navy and Air Force increased both spending and the number of facilities in the San Francisco and San Diego areas. The Cold War increased fears of a nuclear attack on mainland US, and the electronics war eventually moved into space with the development of satellite surveillance (see Chapter 4).

Electronics companies proliferated around the San Francisco and Palo Alto areas, and until the mid-1970s most technology companies in the region were dependent on military contracts. Government had provided the R&D, the equipment contracts, the personnel training and the test-bedding which fuelled the development of budding technologies from radios to vacuum tubes through to semiconductors and integrated circuits, and then to computing equipment and technologies. Of particular importance was the role the military played in Silicon Valley through the funding of young technology companies with innovations during their first 5 years. Professor Stephen Adams describes how time and time again early technology companies of Silicon Valley and the San Francisco Bay area were supported by federal defence contracts. These included the Federal Telegraph Company (radio networks), Eitel-McCullough (radar equipment), Hewlett-Packard (electronic instruments), Ampex (recording equipment), Varian (microwave tubes) and Fairfield Semiconductors, among many others. The defence contracts provided the revenue and reduced the risk in the early stages of technology commercialisation.

> What did individual companies receive in exchange for meeting the military's needs? Time. Scholars of entrepreneurship have found that half of all start-ups fail during their first five years, and that, for various reasons (such as learning curve),

casualty rates drop considerably during subsequent years. The collective challenge faced during the first five years, known as the 'liability of newness,' is one reason for the popularity of start-up incubators. The idea is that if it has support during a particularly vulnerable period, the fledgling company will later be able to build the relationships, pipeline of products, and organization necessary to stand on its own. During the period 1909–1959, defence contracts not only helped sustain Silicon Valley start-ups during their formative years, but allowed them to grow rapidly (Adams 2021, p. 18).

Lemelson Center historian Dr Eric Hintz also synthesises points made by Kenney (2000, pp. 48–67) and Lecuyer (2006) in stating:

> Thus, the military essentially subsidised most technological innovation in the valley's burgeoning electronics industry
>   ...the Department of Defense was the valley's original 'angel' investor and an ideal client.
>   ... long before the valley's first semiconductor firms emerged in the 1950s and 1960s, the region's pioneering electronics firms had already developed the technical and managerial skills necessary to introduce and commercialize new innovations (Hintz 2015).

Although there were several supportive key personnel in the development of Silicon Valley, the cluster would not have existed without large defence contracts to early-stage electronics companies from the beginning of the 20th century to the 1970s. Many of the firms supported by defence contracts were based in Silicon Valley and attracted by both the funding and proximity to naval personnel and facilities that used the technologies. Again, the focus was sharply on the technology rather than who provided it. Much of the development stayed nearby and was further commercialised for civilian and other purposes. Put simply, government procurement focused on progressing technologies of potential built the world-leading ICT cluster that is now known as Silicon Valley.

Table 6.1. Advantages and disadvantages of technology-led innovation efforts

Advantages	Disadvantages
• Technology-led innovation can leverage government spending to develop new technologies and build local technology clusters. Technology-led innovation has built some of the world's largest and most innovative technology clusters, including Silicon Valley. • Technology-led innovation can modernise public services and improve efficiency through cost reduction or better services. • Contracts with local technology developers can build collaborations and partnerships – particularly between research, government and industry partners. • Government contracts for technology-led innovation can provide early-stage businesses with market validation and experience, funding through their 'valley of death' period, and greater knowledge of the needs of the government sector.	• Implementing new technology and systems can be high-risk. A number may not achieve the outcomes they set out to achieve or their costs may blow out. The risk is reduced if there are competent project managers who undertake risk assessments and phased introduction of services. Tests in sandpits, innovation laboratories and public sector observatories may also assist in reducing the risk before the rollout of a new technology. • New systems may be developed before protocols for the industry are established. This means that technology may need to be upgraded or replaced a short time after it is developed. • Free-trade and other agreements restricting government procurement may make it difficult to procure for new technologies from small or local providers. Schemes such as the Small Business Innovation Research (SBIR) in the US and its UK analogue create dedicated funding pools for innovative products and services. • Funding needs to be dedicated to technology development or modernisation and this may take resources away from other important areas of government services.

Successful technology-led innovation effort: Estonian blockchain industry

Blockchain is just the latest in Estonia's rapid public adoption and utilisation of new online technologies. This has occurred through a policy of modernisation that has seen Estonia become a technological leader in e-government over last three decades. Modernisation of the Estonian public sector has been used to build new export industries in its private sector. According to the e-Estonia website (2020), 5.9 per cent of workers in Estonia work in ICT industries, there have been over 1000 ICT startups since 2011 with four of those becoming unicorns (companies worth over US$1 billion. Over 99 per cent of all public services are now available to citizens online (e-Estonia 2020).

When Estonia, with its tiny population of just under 1.5 million, gained independence from the USSR in 1990, it was a comparatively poor and a technologically lagging state. The newly formed government immediately looked to digital technology to develop new and more efficient public services and jump-start a democratic economy. The government started with the provision of high-bandwidth services to the entire population and ensured universal services, with cheap access in regional and rural areas. The government also focused on equipping schools, libraries and public access points with computing hardware, even before fixing playgrounds and buildings. Free wifi hotspots were also provisioned for public spaces across the nation.

Estonia claims to have been using blockchain since 2008 when it developed its 'X-Road' decentralised distributed information system. This was the same year the world's first blockchain, Bitcoin, was described in its now famous White Paper.

In 2012, just 3 years after the launch of Bitcoin and long before any other government applications, the Estonian Ministry of Justice put their entire Succession Registry records onto a blockchain (PriceWaterhouseCoopers 2019). Lessons were learned from these initial applications on how to use and store data records in relation to speed, immutability and scalability. Estonia then investigated using blockchain for healthcare records and became the first country in the world to use blockchain in a national public record system:

> 'We are using blockchain as an additional layer of security to help us ensure the integrity of health records. Privacy and integrity of healthcare information are a top priority for the government and we are happy to work with innovative technologies like the blockchain to make sure our records are kept safe,' said Artur Novek, the foundation's Implementation Manager and Architect (Einaste 2018).

Blockchain-based data protection on the X-Road system in Estonia now underpins almost all government services.

> Today state services ranging from tax to e-Health plus private sector service providers utilise the system [X-Road]. Blockchain usage is invisible to users yet the benefits are proven, ultra-high security, data immutability and 800 years of time savings annually. With such unique proof of concept, it is unsurprising that Estonia is at the forefront of the emerging Blockchain economy (Invest in Estonia 2020).

Estonia has been the birthplace of Guardtime, reportedly the world's largest blockchain company platform (Invest in Estonia 2020). Other Estonian blockchain companies have flourished in cryptocurrency, real estate, startup investment and communications. The Estonian government has also become a

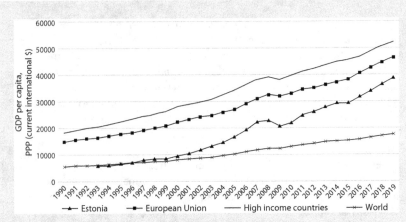

Fig. 6.3.   Estonia GSP per capita (PPP). Source: World Bank.

leading advisor on e-government development to other governments around the world. The e-Estonia Briefing Centre has hosted over 4700 delegations since 2009, including those from 130 countries.

The rapid modernisation of Estonia through e-government initiatives has seen Estonia's GDP grow rapidly. Between 1993 and 2018, GDP per capita (PPP) in Estonia rose by 620 per cent – from under $6000 dollars per person in 1993 to over $36 000 in 2018 (Fig. 6.3). This economic transformation has been led by government modernisation, which has not only created new and efficient government services, but has also developed skills and built local export industries.

Case study: Less successful technology-led innovation effort

Development of the drone industry in Queensland

In 2012 organisers of the Unmanned Aerial Vehicles (UAV) Outback Challenge – a competitive drone event in western Queensland, Australia – wrote to the Queensland State Government's Department of Innovation. The organisers of the event asked if the government could consider how newly developed drones might assist in government work.

The authors of the letter requested a time to present on the new capabilities of drones to a high-level, cross-departmental committee (Heads of Departments or Chief Information Officers). In their letter they suggested a few applications that might be considered: surveying powerlines and remote infrastructure, monitoring environmental conditions, or assessing damage in natural disasters such as floods and fires. The organisers of the UAV Challenge (originally three scientists and researchers from a local university and the CSIRO – Australia's national science agency) also suggested that more applications could come to light if they had the opportunity to discuss the technology with government officers and find out more about their work. Drones could be co-developed with government agencies and new technologies trialled. Contracts with government, they wrote, would be one of the best ways to support the emerging Queensland UAV industry. Government contracts would provide market legitimacy and funding, and encourage operators and developers to create new products for customised applications. After all, the organisers' motivation for the UAV Outback Challenge had been to 'assist in bringing UAVs into common place use in non-military domains' (UAV Challenge 2021).

In 2012, however, UAVs were still expensive and not considered part of everyday government operations, and regulation on their use was still being considered by air safety authorities. This would change over the next 10 years as protocols for their use were developed and government officers read more about the use of drones in government work elsewhere. Slowly government officers saw how they could create great efficiencies by cutting costs and improving services.

While the Queensland Department of Innovation sponsored the UAV Outback Challenge in 2012, the presentation to departmental heads on the capabilities of drones did not eventuate at that time. The letter was referred on to other mid-level officers in other departments but, as with many governments, there was no overarching 'open door' for industry and academia to pitch new technology. In some cases, new technologies were pitched directly to the Chief Innovation Officer (CIO), but this was usually at the request of the CIO and in relation to specifically identified needs. This process mostly involved comparing relatively developed technologies offered by large IT firms, such as cloud computing services and cybersecurity options.

Since 2012, the Queensland drone industry has grown considerably. The 2018 Queensland Drone Strategy estimated that more than 30 per cent of the Australian drone industry was based in Queensland (Queensland Government 2018). Drones, including UAVs, are now being used extensively in agriculture, mining, emergency services, the entertainment and photography industry and by local councils (Fig. 6.4). This isn't a story of completely missed opportunity. However, the development of new drone technologies and applications could perhaps have grown a lot faster, and gained more of a world-leading edge, had developers who were making their own machines back in 2012 received early interest from government and gained early-stage government contracts for the use of UAVs in government operations.

Fig. 6.4. Fully autonomous drone from Emesent with a Hovermap system. Photo credit: Katrina Lo Surdo, CSIRO.

Summary

Taking a technology-led approach leverages public sector procurement spending to advance technologies and build local industries in emerging technology. It can be a two-for-one deal, building new industries at the same time as cutting costs to government and providing more efficient public services. The key to building new industries through technology-led innovation is having skilled government officials who have a deep understanding of emerging technology, and who can manage a project effectively and safely introduce a new technology to public sector settings. This may be through testing laboratories, proof-of-concept trials, public sector observatories, regulatory sandpits or in partnerships with research organisations. Technology-led innovation has both caused the greatest embarrassment to governments and created the greatest innovation hotspots in the world.

Endnote

[1] Compiled with primary research and assistance from Dr Eric Hintz, Senior Historian from the Lemelson Center at the Smithsonian National Museum of American History, and Professor Stephen Adams from Salisbury University, Maryland, US.

References

Adams SB (2021) From orchards to chips: Silicon Valley's evolving entrepreneurial ecosystem. *Entrepreneurship & Regional Development* **33**, 15–35. doi.org/10.1080/08985626.2020.1734259

Blank S (2008) *The Hidden History of Silicon Valley.* <https://www.youtube.com/watch?v=ZTC_RxWN_xo>

Cameron A, Hintz E, Bedi J, Smith M, Adams S (unpublished) Can Governments create an innovation hot spot? Report for the Queensland Government from Smithsonian Fellow Dr Lucy Cameron 2015.

Candelon F, Reeves M, Wu D (2018) 18 of the top 20 tech companies are in the Western U.S. and Eastern China. Can anywhere else catch up? *Harvard Business Review*, 3 May.

Charette RN (2019) Five enduring government IT failures: costly consequences go on and on. *IEEE Spectrum*, 5 February. <https://spectrum.ieee.org/five-enduring-government-it-failures>

Companies Market Cap (2021) *Largest companies by market cap.* <https://companiesmarketcap.com/>

e-Estonia (2020) We have built a digital society and we can show you how. e-Estonia briefing centre. E-Estonia, Tallinn. <https://e-estonia.com/>

Einaste T (2018) Blockchain and healthcare: the Estonian experience. Nortal, Helsinki, 21 February. <https://nortal.com/us/blog/blockchain-healthcare-estonia/>

Hintz E (2015) Suburban Garage Hackers + Lab Researchers = Personal Computing. In *Places of Invention: A companion to the exhibition at the Smithsonian's National Museum of American History.* (Eds AP Molella, A Karvellas) pp. 14–41. Smithsonian Institution Scholarly Press, Washington DC.

Homeland Security News Wire (2010) Why SBINet has failed. *Homeland Security News Wire*, Mineloa. 19 May. <https://www.homelandsecuritynewswire.com/why-sbinet-has-failed>

Invest in Estonia (2020) Blockchain. The Estonian Investment Agency,Tallinn <https://investinestonia.com/business-opportunities/blockchain/>

Justinia T (2017) The UK's National Programme for IT: why was it dismantled? *Health services management research* **30**, 2–9. doi:10.1177/0951484816662492

Kenney M (2000) *Understanding Silicon Valley: The anatomy of an entrepreneurial region.* Stanford University Press, Stanford.

Lecuyer C (2006) *Making Silicon Valley: Innovation and the growth of high tech, 1930–1970.* MIT Press, Cambridge, Massachusetts.

Lemelson Center for the Study of Invention and Innovation (2014) *Places of Invention Exhibition: Overview.* Smithsonian National Museum of American History. <https://invention.si.edu/places-invention-exhibition-overview>

Molella AP, Karvellas A (Eds) (2015) *Places of Invention: A companion to the exhibition at the Smithsonian's National Museum of American History.* Smithsonian Institution Scholarly Press, Washington DC.

OECD (2017) *Public Procurement for Innovation: Good practices and strategies.* OECD, Paris.

Pitchbook, NVCA (2020) *Venture Monitor Q4 2020.* Pitchbook NVCA, Seattle. <https://files.pitchbook.com/website/files/pdf/Q4_2020_PitchBook_NVCA_Venture_Monitor.pdf>

PriceWaterhouseCoopers (2019) *Estonia – the digital republic secured by Blockchain.* PriceWaterhouseCoopers, Tallinn. <https://www.pwc.com/gx/en/services/legal/tech/assets/estonia-the-digital-republic-secured-by-blockchain.pdf>

Queensland Government (2018) Queensland Drone Strategy. Queensland Government, Brisbane, Australia.

Shahady D (2019) Foreword. In *SBIR|STTR 2019 A Year in Review.* US Air Force, Austin, Texas.

Small Business Innovation Research (2020) About SBIR. <https://www.sbir.gov/about/>

Sturgeon TJ (2000) How Silicon Valley came to be. In *Understanding Silicon Valley: The Anatomy of an Entrepreneurial Region.* (Ed. M Kenney) pp. 15–47. Stanford University Press, Stanford, California.

Subcommittee on Technology and Innovation (2009) The role of the SBIR and STTR programs in stimulating innovation at small high-tech businesses. Hearing of the Subcommittee on Technology and Innovation, Committee on Science and Technology. US Government, Washington, DC.

UAV Challenge (2021) *About us.* UAV Challenge. <uavchallenge.org/about>

US Air Force (2019) *SBIR|STTR – 2019 A year in review.* US Air Force, Austin, Texas.

Willis R (2015) 4 massive Australian IT project failures and why they failed. Your Project Manager, Brisbane, 29 December. <https://yourprojectmanager.com.au/4-massive-australian-project-failures-failed/>

7

The future of innovation

The future of innovation is not a brief topic. There are multiple futures that can occur, depending on our ability to create and develop technologies and control their uses. To consider the future of innovation we need to examine current trajectories, the new emerging technologies and ways in which they may be used. The following is as simplified an overview as can be provided in a short chapter, but it is in no way a comprehensive or detailed coverage of the topic; there is so much revolutionary technology being developed in 2021, and not all of it is described here. To help structure the complex landscape ahead, I will use foresight techniques to break down the future innovation landscape into the main drivers of change, or megatrends.

2020 – the great reset

'Necessity is the mother of all invention' is the adage, and nothing makes innovation more necessary than a threat to our survival. When it comes to facing existential threats, humans are practised at using our big brains and our ability to collaborate and utilise resources to fast-track our invention processes and find survival mechanisms.

In 2020, the human race faced an existential threat in the form of a global pandemic. It spurred and tested our collective innovation systems to find vaccines in record time and implement novel infection control methods along the way. This could not have been done without new platform technologies, innovative digital twins and visualisations of the virus structure, global collaborations and shared infrastructure.

The COVID-19 pandemic took its toll. At the time of writing (October 2021) there have been over 4.8 million deaths and over 235 million cases worldwide. Although the death and infection numbers have shocked the world and left many families grieving, 123 vaccines have gone to clinical trials and eight effective and separate vaccines have been developed and tested by medical teams around the world for widespread use – all within 12 months (World Health Organization 2021a). Prior to the COVID-19 pandemic, a typical vaccine would take 5–10 years to develop (Coronavirus Research Center JHU 2021), but within 20 months of the first cases being reported in Wuhan, China, in late 2019, over 6.2 billion doses of vaccines have been administered and global cases are falling (Johns Hopkins University 2021; World Health Organization 2021b). With new variants of the virus emerging every few months, however, it remains to be seen how effective our vaccine controls will be in the longer term.

The COVID-19 and other pandemics are not the only foreseeable threat we are going to face over the next few decades. As the world warms, we also face the necessity of bringing down atmospheric carbon dioxide before it creates more unliveable environments and pushes many of our fellow species to extinction. In 2019, the United Nations warned that species decline is accelerating and the planet will lose over 1 million species over the coming decades unless our interactions with wild places change (IPBES 2019). We also face an overpopulated world of dwindling resources. This may trigger political tensions and possibly even armed conflict. It is no accident that innovation and defence spending are often linked. Survival is also a matter of economics and value capture, and these will also be challenged with the implementation and deployment of digital currencies, blockchain contracts, new funding mechanisms and updated intellectual property systems.

The 2020 COVID-19 pandemic has now repeatedly been referred to as 'the great reset' (Ede 2020; Schwab 2020). By locking down national populations across the globe, it has drastically impacted the way we live, work and distribute global resources. The pandemic may also have reset the way and places in which we undertake innovation,

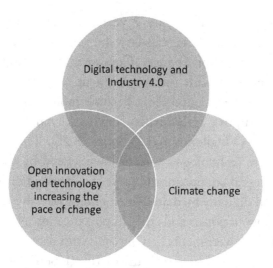

Fig. 7.1. Drivers of change in the future of innovation.

due to an acceleration in three existing megatrends driving future change (Fig. 7.1):

1. the next wave of digital technology, often referred to as 'Industry 4.0'
2. climate change, creating an imperative for technological solutions
3. the increased pace of innovation, creating a move towards 'open innovation' and open-source software.

The new wave of digital technologies (Industry 4.0)

In 1890, classical economist Alfred Marshall (1890) stated: 'Every cheapening of the means of communication, every new facility for the free interchange of ideas between distant places alters the action of the forces which tend to localise industries.' Marshall wrote these words just a few years after Alexander Bell had submitted his patent for a telephone in 1876 and created the Bell Telephone Company in 1877. Over 130 years later, Marshall's words remain prescient.

We are on the verge of an explosion in digital technologies that are altering the geography of human interactions and the interchange of ideas. Moore's law, which states that the number of transistors on a computer chip will double every 2 years, has held true over the last 50 years – increasing the capacity for computer processing and quickening the pace of change. Computer processing is likely to accelerate even faster with the development of quantum computing. Digital data flows have reportedly become more valuable than oil or gold and are disrupting and restructuring traditional value systems (*The Economist* 2017; O'Halloran and D'Souza 2020). The shift to digital and use of these technologies was also accelerated by the COVID-19 pandemic as digital connections became the lifeblood of workplaces.

Virtual and digitally mediated interaction spaces are replacing some face-to-face interactions, and the importance of physical place is changing. For governments trying to stimulate innovation and economic activity within strict jurisdictional boundaries, capturing innovative activity and the value from that activity seems to have become a slippery concept. Legacy legal systems regulating intellectual property, managers who believe in productivity in the office and the clusters of venture capital firms investing in new companies and wanting face-to-face contact with managers of their investments appear to be holding the old world together. That may be changing in the new global landscape shaped by Industry 4.0 technologies, including:

- blockchain, including cryptocurrencies
- augmented and virtual reality (AR/VR)
- artificial intelligence (AI)
- 3D printing and additive manufacturing
- robotics and drone technologies using GPS and geospatial technology from sensor networks
- the Internet of Things (IoT)
- human–cyber integration
- quantum computing
- increases in the use of platforms enabled by better broadband networks, data storage and cloud applications.

These technologies can be used in isolation or in various combinations. They will impact not just the geography of innovation, but the security and value of information, institutions creating new products and services, the way innovation is funded and distributed, and the meaning of innovation itself.

Advances in distributed and renewable energy (solar panels, wind and tidal generators and new storage technology) may also impact where this next generation of technologies is able to be deployed. Below are just a few examples of how this next wave of digital technologies may impact the geography of innovation, and the changing ability of governments to build innovation hotspots over the next decade.

Digital technologies are providing locational freedom for many more workers

The COVID-19 pandemic lockdowns forced many companies to implement work-from-home practices. Working from home had been slowly increasing since the 1970s, accelerating markedly since the 2000s when it was enabled by the internet, email, laptops and smartphones. At the end of 2019 (and the beginning of the pandemic), in Australia alone around 24 per cent of the workforce undertook part of their work duties from a place other than their usual office. This figure had almost doubled to 41 per cent by February 2021 (Australian Bureau of Statistics 2021), and early indicators suggest that many workers will not be returning to their previous routines of being in the office 5 days a week after the pandemic ends (Broom 2021).

Although workers had the ability to work from home before the pandemic, the practice had mostly only been taken up by senior staff, independent knowledge workers and those required to travel as part of their work duties. For most employees, the prospect of working away from their offices remained largely theoretical until the COVID-19 pandemic made it a necessity (Choudhury 2020).

In 2020, the use of team videoconferencing software (applications such as Zoom, Microsoft Teams, Google Hangouts and CISCO's Webex) suddenly skyrocketed – taken up by workers, school groups, social groups, business networks and higher educational institutions. The share price for the previously relatively unknown company Zoom Video Communications rose over 800 per cent from US$66 in October 2019 to US$575 in October 2020 – where it peaked after announcements of the successful human trials of the first Pfizer and AstraZeneca vaccines were reported.

The locational freedom and sharp rise in video conferencing also impacted property markets. Throughout 2020, property prices rose sharply in regional lifestyle locations, which were nicknamed 'Zoom Boom' towns in the media (Fig. 7.2) (Rosalsky 2020; Johanson 2021). According to the Pew Research Center, 3 per cent of American adults moved permanently or temporarily due to the COVID-19 pandemic (Cohn 2020).

Harvard researcher Prithwiraj Choudhury (2020) suggests that the permanent impacts of the locational freedom enabled by the increased take-up of work-from-home/work-from-anywhere practices will create new innovation patterns. This is because it has changed access to skilled labour and also because working remotely will create new interaction spaces essential for sharing ideas and creating knowledge spillovers.

By bringing their work with them, people will be able to live where it is most desirable: where it's most affordable, close to family, where they can access necessary health facilities, or stay with a spouse who

Fig. 7.2. A beach in the city of Hobart, Tasmania. Hobart has been one of the 'Zoom Boom' towns in Australia, with house prices rising 12 per cent in 2020. Source: CoreLogic.

has had to move for their job. Skilled employees may be able to stay longer with the same organisation instead of resigning due to a relocation as they may have had to in the past. This may make it easier for organisations to retain skilled workers, particularly women who are often the first to give up their jobs when their partners need to relocate or when they have a family.

It will also mean that companies can more easily hire from a global talent pool. Before the COVID-19 pandemic, they may have been limited by the availability of locally trained staff. A remote university, for instance, can now consider employing someone in statistics who lives in another state or, indeed, another country, without asking them to come onto campus at all. The effort to import skilled staff through difficult visa programs and relocation schemes may be alleviated by simply employing more staff in-situ in their own regions and countries.

The winners of greater locational freedom for workers will be lifestyle regions, and also countries with highly skilled but lower-wage workforces. Workers in countries such as India, Vietnam, China and Kenya may start to receive greater work opportunities from companies headquartered in higher-wage countries. These low-wage countries have traditionally suffered from a 'brain drain', as educated individuals are given job offers and poached for higher paying and skilled jobs elsewhere. The offshoring that first occurred in manufacturing work will continue into the professions.

Lifestyle towns in the US have started offering cash and other incentives for knowledge-workers to move in, setting up co-working centres with fast broadband and meeting rooms, along with providing active lifestyle options such as hiking, cycling and boating (Johanson 2021).

The geographic dispersal of workers post-COVID will also affect the places and times we have incidental interactions with other people, interactions that often spark new innovations. Instead of casual and opportunistic conversations at the watercooler, in the elevator, at the coffee cart or in communal kitchens that spark innovative activities between individuals *within* an organisation, there may be more casual conversations with people *outside* the firm while hiking, mountain-biking or walking the dog on the beach. That may make capturing intellectual property within the firm harder, or it might increase the likelihood of more information being brought in from outside. Studies are needed to add data to these questions.

Incidental and relatively random interactions within organisations may also be digitally reconstructed. For example, Choudhury describes an experimental digital program that simulated random incidental interactions in what he described as a 'virtual watercooler conversation.' An algorithm would randomly schedule meetings between people from all levels of a firm (Choudhury *et al.* 2020; Bojinov *et al.* 2021). The experiment found that interns in a large global firm that had randomised opportunities to interact with senior managers were more likely to get offers of employment. Senior managers also gained insights into the work being done at more operational levels (Bojinov *et al.* 2021). As workforces disperse and interact more digitally, people may also meet and share ideas in social interest groups on corporate platforms. Our research organisation, for instance, has internal staff groups to post and share tips and photos on our pets and hobbies.

Social networks, such as Facebook, LinkedIn and Instagram, have already enabled users to increasingly keep up with people located around the world. Friends groups and connections are more likely to be historical or based on interest groups instead of being just geographically close. Work contacts may be following the same trajectory, and in terms of innovation this may change how regions can both attract and retain their skilled workers and stimulate local economic activity.

Virtual clusters and hubs

The dispersal of workers across large distances is likely to stimulate policy and organisations to support virtual hubs or expertise clusters instead of physical ones. Australia's national research agency, CSIRO, has been an example of how digital networks and collaboration platforms can enable scientific project teams from across the large continent to form quickly around missions, challenges or specific pieces of work, mostly without the need for physical co-location. CSIRO has over 5000 employees at 53 sites across Australia, and three international sites. Multidisciplinary teams quickly come together for projects and tasks. Physical infrastructure and equipment are located at certain sites, but much of this is able to be accessed by staff working away from the site. Film production studios also often have global teams that 'follow the sun' or work around the clock due to being placed in different time zones. A virtual hub might contain specific access to digital assets or collaboration tools or may, in the near future, be a place created in virtual reality.

Augmented reality and virtual reality (AR/VR) are creating new virtual meeting and training spaces

AR/VR are assisting this locational freedom by rapidly changing everything from education experiences to the creation of virtual meeting spaces. Although still clunky at times and not ever quite living up to the promise of many depictions in science fiction films such as *Ready Player One*, the technology is getting closer to creating environments that mimic real-life interactions for the purposes of gaming, meetings, shopping and business gatherings. Facebook (Meta) and Apple are investing heavily in new standalone VR headsets (Oculus Quest and Apple VR), Microsoft is further developing its AR/VR platform (Hololens) for a variety of applications, Google is developing mobile-phone-based applications (Google Lens).

Perhaps some of the largest benefits of augmented and virtual reality have been, and will be, in training – an area that has long benefited from flight simulators and biomedical haptics. This will mean that doctors, for instance, can competently and safely be trained in more surgeries before operating on a real person. And they can also be trained and supported anywhere in the world. Augmented reality software can assist by providing an information overlay to real-life vision. Existing applications include showing where veins are as a needle is being inserted, providing blood pressure measurements, monitoring hygiene and showing what to operate on. These applications will be expanded over the coming decades to enable far greater levels of remote training, monitoring, hygienic hospital practice and surgery. Augmented reality applications already work with scanners and diagnostic AI programs to instantly recognise medical anomalies and diagnose conditions or send measurements to 3D printers to create on-the-spot bone supports or skin grafts.

Global research platforms that have created digital models of the COVID-19 molecule and other viruses have been vital in the development of vaccines for the pandemic. These have been globally distributed and teams around the world have worked on disabling various parts of the virus in order to develop immune responses and vaccines.

Digital twins – whereby a 3D, digital replica of a person, city or an environment is re-created and monitored – enable scientific teams situated all around the world to collaborate to solve problems and engineer solutions (Fig. 7.3). Farming and mining operations can all be done from headquarters in cities or towns hundreds or thousands of kilometres away, through a combination of robotics, AI, the Internet of Things, sensor networks, GPS and satellite technology, and fast broadband networks. Remotely driven trucks, trains, drilling equipment, farm gates, watering points and mineral scanning

Fig. 7.3. The NSW Spatial Digital Twin of Western Sydney, Australia, uses 3D imagery along with 3D models of live buses and train movements (from the NSW Department of Customer Service and Transport for NSW respectively), along with hundreds of other Open, Shared and Closed datasets from Australian governments of all levels, to create a mixed reality landscape.

technology are already in use in advanced mines and farms around the world.

In March 2021, the US Army awarded Microsoft a $22 billion contract to develop smart headsets using augmented reality to deliver 'next generation night vision and situational awareness' (Fig. 7.4). These will allow soldiers to train, rehearse and fight using a single platform. 'The system leverages augmented reality and machine learning to enable a life-like mixed reality training environment' (US Army Program Executive Office Soldier 2021). Theoretically, soldiers using these headsets could train anywhere in the world.

Augmented and virtual reality (mixed reality) programs are also being used in entertainment, real estate, construction and tourism, allowing workers, investors, visitors and planners to immerse themselves in an environment (or planned environment) before going there, or working or investing in the industry.

Augmented and virtual reality, fast broadband, team videoconferencing, robotics and sensor networks and the Internet of Things are making

Fig. 7.4. A US Army soldier tests Microsoft Hololens configured as the Integrated Visual Augmentation System (IVAS). Public domain image by Sgt Kaitlyn Klein.

remote work available for far greater types of work, and working, training and collaborating globally are becoming more common and available to more people.

New levels of crowdfunding and crowdsourcing innovation via platforms

In 2011, I was asked to write a ministerial brief on crowdfunding for new product development. Platforms such as Indiegogo and Kickstarter (launched in 2008 and 2009 respectively) were starting to cause excitement in the local entrepreneur and startup community. Government regulators were unsure how to view investment via crowdfunding platforms – whether they would operate under consumer law (as if people were buying products and services), donations to good causes (like a charity), shares in an enterprise (like an investment) or be recorded as tax-deductible investment in research and development (R&D). (Answer: in Australia, crowdfunding can be classed as any of these things depending on what sort of contribution a person makes and the platform used.)

Since that time, however, crowdfunding platforms have grown to be a significant contributor to new product development around the world and their use is still expanding. The crowdfunding market was calculated to be worth between US$14.2–40 billion in 2019 and is estimated to expand 11–18 per cent in compound annual growth (CAGR) over the next 5 years (The startups team 2018; Mordor Intelligence 2020; Technavio 2020). Some predict the crowdfunding market will be worth $300 billion by 2026 (The startups team 2018). Interestingly, Startups.com reports that the North American market – where the largest crowdfunding platforms originated – are not the main users or contributors to crowdfunding. The smaller markets of South America, Oceania (including Australia, New Zealand and the Pacific Islands) and Africa all raise more funds for projects via crowdfunding sites than the North American market. This perhaps illustrates that the opportunity for getting new products to market is shifting and opening up through these global platforms. It may also indicate that the lack of more established venture capital investment in these smaller markets makes crowdfunding one of the few means for individuals to fund new product development.

Cryptocurrency funding

More recently, the crowdfunding market has been supplemented with a global surge in investment in cryptocurrency. Bitcoin, launched in 2009 as a response to the Global Financial Crisis, was the world's first cryptocurrency. The last 5 years have seen the cryptocurrency markets explode in both value and diversity. In January 2015, the total market capitalisation for all cryptocurrency was estimated to be $5.4 billion, mostly held in two coins: Bitcoin and Ethereum. By mid-2021, the total market capitalisation of the cryptocurrency markets had reached US$1.72 trillion, which was distributed across thousands of cryptocurrencies (Coin360 2021). New products and organisations – particularly in fintech but also energy and water markets, information networks, utilities, health, entertainment, foreign aid, property and legal sectors – have all been developed and funded via cryptocurrency tokens. In many cases, the cryptocurrency token is the product, but in many more cases, the tokens are funding the transactions and the development of new global trading systems and a reorganisation of distribution in digital and other commodities.

Blockchain technology more generally (the technology behind cryptocurrency) may fundamentally alter the way value is transmitted over digital networks, in some cases replacing other forms of fiat currency (Tapscott and Tapscott 2016). Thus, blockchain can alter the geography of innovation through the internationalisation of investment at a scale not previously imagined. Cryptocurrencies are usually sold globally, and can be bought, sold and transmit value without many of the charges associated with trading across borders and institutions.

Several crowdfunding platforms are now accepting cryptocurrency as pledges of support or as equity contributions. Cryptocurrencies and platforms that support new ventures (beyond their own new business) are starting to support each other (Matthews 2018).

Theta and its TFUEL token

Theta Laboratories, Inc., has set out to create the world's first decentralised video streaming and delivery network powered by a cryptocurrency token. Its developers hope to fundamentally disrupt the world of centralised, one-to-many video streaming services. Video streaming services have grown rapidly with the deployment of faster broadband networks and currently use most of the available bandwidth, often slowing regional or peripheral networks. Users of the Theta Network will be able to earn tokens (named TFUEL) by sharing and relaying videos (peer-to-peer), creating higher quality streaming and providing more localisation and less centralisation in the delivery of video for entertainment (sports, TV and movies):

> *Video streaming is a continually growing industry as more people across the world have access to streaming devices. The overall architecture [of Theta] benefits both users and video streaming platforms. Users can earn tokens for sharing their bandwidth, and also get to be part of a community, while content creators and platforms lower streaming costs on their part (McCormack 2020).*

With a governance council that includes executives from Google, Samsung, Sony and the US Creative Artists Agency (CAA), Theta has sparked interest from the crypto investor market. Sales of TFUEL tokens have already been issued on global cryptocurrency exchanges and in mid-2021 had a market cap of US\$3.4 billion while Theta tokens (a separate governance token) had a market cap of US\$9.6 billion. This money has been invested before the network and business model is even operational (Palmer 2021).

NFTs

One of the ways blockchain is changing the systems of value transfer is through non-fungible tokens (NFTs). These are blockchain-based digital labels that are attached to digital products (artworks, memes, digital titles), so they can be authenticated and traded securely across the internet ('fungible' means tradable for similar value). A viral digital meme, for example, may be authenticated with an NFT and this can then be sold to someone who would like to own that part of cultural history. Jack Dorsey, founder of Twitter, recently sold his first tweet ('just setting up my twttr') as an NFT for \$2.9 million.

NFTs hold the promise of stimulating artistic and other digital content through incentivising funding for their creation. Again, these digital products could occur anywhere and enrich artistic communities around the globe. A darker side to NFTs is that they may also be facilitating money laundering and tax evasion. The digital art attached to an NFT often has a highly subjective market value and can be used to convert illegal funds into recordable losses (Loizos 2021).

Artificial intelligence (AI) and picking innovation winners

The impacts of AI are also changing not just the geography of innovation, but the definition of innovation itself.

As optimisation programs, machine learning and natural language processing (the core of AI) get to work on problems and provide innovative solutions, they often adapt both human and their own machine behaviours (i.e. they learn from environments and they can also modify behaviours). One of the more groundbreaking uses of AI in science is in predicting 3D protein structures with high atomic accuracy from their amino acid sequence. This can be used to transform medical research in areas including research into vaccines and drug treatments (Callaway 2021; Service 2021). Questions are starting to be asked about whether AI programs should be able to own patents (Skaff et al. 2020; Tapscott 2020), be assigned rights akin to sentient beings (AI Rights Institute 2021) or determine which innovative ideas have the most potential and are funded (Council 2021). Could AI create and fund innovation itself?

For now, AI programs cannot own patents – a landmark US Patents and Trademark Office (USPTO) ruling has stated that a patent holder must be human (Skaff et al. 2020; Tapscott 2020), and they are not yet considered to be sentient beings in regards to human-like rights. AI *is* starting to impact the investment decisions of venture capital firms, however, and this will determine where new firms are funded and where innovation occurs.

The research and consulting company Gartner predicts that AI will be used to make or assist in investment decisions in up to 75 per cent of large venture capital firms by 2025, up from around 5 per cent today (Council 2021; Rimol and Costello 2021). The geographic impact of the increasing use of AI in funding innovation is unclear, but I personally fear it may promote and enlarge existing geographic innovation clusters. Data patterns studied by AI algorithms in order to make predictions are often historical, so previous success factors (e.g. being located in Silicon Valley) may determine which firms the programs think will succeed in the future. It may also be more likely to fund people who have previously been successful in bringing new innovative ventures to market.

The impact of AI in *where* innovation occurs will really depend on the weightings of the contributing success factors within the algorithm. That is, how much the AI algorithm considers the location of a firm contributed to its success, in relation to other factors such as the product/service being created, the likely disruption caused by the innovation or new business model, and the team behind its development. Innovation is one of those ground-shifting areas, however, where historical data can sometimes be completely irrelevant to the success of the venture. The young entrepreneurs who created and managed Google, Facebook and Twitter may never have been funded based on historical data.

However, there is no doubt that AI will play an increasing role in the venture capital and investment industry. Along with AI being used increasingly by venture capitalists, it is also being adopted in assessments of R&D funding applications to improve productivity and gain greater return on investment for expenditure (Fleming *et al.* 2017; Surae 2018). Prioritisation of new industry support in trade and economic development may also adopt similar machine-learning assistance (Hajkowicz *et al.* 2020). Although these are early days, advanced data sciences and AI are starting to infiltrate decision-making in all areas investing in innovation as people attempt to de-risk their investments and pick more winners. This is bound to impact the geography of innovation and the success or otherwise of emerging innovation hotspots.

3D printing and additive manufacturing

The COVID-19 pandemic and subsequent disruption to global trade refocused attention on sovereign manufacturing capability and manufacturing flexibility. 'Pivoting' in 2020 was the essential skill for many businesses forced to close down production on traditional items and open up production in others. For instance, because no one was allowed in bars for months, a gin distillery close to my home stopped making gin and started producing alcohol-based hand-sanitiser, which was in short supply. To pivot effectively, the distillery changed their production processes and modified their equipment. Adaptable 3D printing, robotics and other 'advanced manufacturing' tools are being touted as options for pivoting industry and the rapid scaling up domestic manufacturing capability in the event of future or sustained global trade restrictions (Pastor 2020).

Early industry assessments suggest the potential to scale up domestic manufacturing or disrupt global value chains using 3D printing varies considerably across industry sectors. It may be useful, for instance, in the production of small-run tools, medical and dental devices, and hard body parts (such as teeth and supports for broken bones), mechanical gadgets and building materials, but not so useful in raw or natural material production, most textiles or paper production, computers or complex electronics, or vehicles (Laplume *et al.* 2016). Large 3D printers are also being trialled in the construction of houses, bridges and office buildings (Hammer 2018). The list of what 3D printing is and isn't useful for may change significantly over the next few years as the technology expands.

What 3D printing and additive manufacturing are assisting in, however, is the rapid prototyping of initial products essential for testing and funding. This is not only because 3D printing can produce a prototype 3D object for people to hold, test and consider, but also because the digitalisation of the design allows collaboration across distances, organisations and countries.

A digital design, necessary to create a 3D prototype, allows testing and rapid modification if needed, slashing the time to create a market-ready product. This rapid prototyping model may also have implications for business model innovation, as businesses using 3D printing technology can rapidly change and adapt to market conditions by adjusting their level of market integration and engagement with the design, manufacturing or distribution of products (Rayna and Striukova 2016).

Basic 3D printers can now be purchased for less than US$500 a unit, and some can be bought in supermarkets (Lambrechts 2016). Although these are not industrial quality and can only use limited materials, they put the ability to tinker, create and collaborate into enthusiasts' homes around the world. They can help innovative ideas materialise in real life.

Climate change is creating a global mission requiring urgent technological solutions

The growing impact of climate change on lives and economies around the world is creating a global imperative that no country can ignore: to bring down the concentrations of atmospheric carbon dioxide (CO_2) and other greenhouse gases before it is too late for many species, perhaps even our own.

Climate change is already causing increases in atmospheric and oceanic temperatures, extreme weather events, droughts and floods, heat waves, rising sea levels, coastal inundation, freshwater shortages, forest and bush fires, and disruption to global biosystems and ecologies affecting our food and other systems. It will only accelerate over the coming decades (IPCC 2019). Our survival as a species depends on finding low- or no-carbon energy sources, carbon-capture and storage technologies, and stabilising altered environments. And we need to do it quickly.

The United Nations Paris Agreement has set a warming target of 1.5°C to mitigate the severest impacts of climate change. To have any chance of achieving this target, carbon emissions have to be cut to zero by 2050 or sooner. Many countries have pledged to cut carbon emissions to zero by 2050, but before the pandemic, few were on track to achieving this (Titley 2017; Nature Climate Change 2021a). But CO_2 isn't the only greenhouse gas that needs to be reduced to fight global warming. Atmospheric methane is also accelerating the global warming process. In addition to human causes of methane emissions such as burning and leaking natural gas, methane is being released into the atmosphere in greater amounts than in the past due to increased microbial activity in the warmer and wetter conditions around the tropics, burning biomass in bush and forest fires as well as melting permafrost, glaciers and icecaps. Worryingly, these are all conditions exacerbated by climate change itself (Schaefer *et al.* 2016; Pearce 2016).

Climate change wasn't accelerated by the COVID-19 pandemic; in fact it was slightly decelerated due to lockdowns temporarily cutting CO_2 emissions from restricted vehicle and air travel (Nature Climate Change 2021b). But in the wake of the pandemic, a sizeable proportion of stimulus funding in many of the world's largest economies is being directed to the shift to renewable energy and the decarbonisation of the global economy (King 2020). The US, China, Canada, France, Germany and the European Union are all directing significant funds from economic stimulus packages towards a transition to renewable energy.

Many are seeing the stimulus funding as an opportunity to tackle climate change faster than ever before and reach the Paris Agreement targets. The International Energy Agency (IEA) believes significant investment in sustainable energy projects post-COVID will mean the globe can avoid the devastating impacts of much higher CO_2 levels and meet its Paris targets, and it has produced encouraging graphs to show how (Fig. 7.5).

Estimates put stimulus spending by governments around the world at over \$19 trillion (Capo-McCormick *et al.* 2021) with a further \$1 trillion projected over each of the next 3 years. Some of that funding has been committed to fossil fuel projects (coal, oil and gas), but the OECD, IEA and other global organisations are promoting the use of stimulus spending to critically accelerate the transition to a decarbonised global economy.

> The SDS [Sustainable Development Scenario] sets out a possible pathway for a very ambitious transformation of the energy sector which incorporates full implementation of existing net-zero pledges for 2050 and earlier (International Energy Agency 2020).

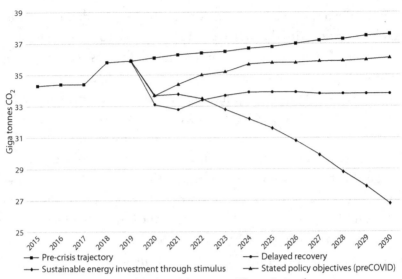

Fig. 7.5. Energy sector and industrial process CO_2 emission by recovery trajectory. Source: International Energy Agency, World Energy Outlook 2020.

The global economy is recovering strongly, with the World Bank forecasting global GDP growth in 2021 at 5.6 per cent, the fastest post-recession recovery in over 80 years. The recovery won't be evenly spread, however, with many emerging economies struggling to recover more than larger, developed economies. It is many of these economies that also need assistance in carbon emissions reductions.

During the COVID-19 pandemic recovery period, there will be an emphasis on new industry and innovation and using the stimulus funding to invest in the technologies for electric vehicles, more efficient energy systems and storage, communications infrastructure and technology, and carbon capture and storage technologies. The 2021 G7 Summit in Cornwall, UK, pledged to support emerging economies transitioning out of a dependence on fossils fuels in the COVID-19 recovery period with $2.8 billion in incentives. They also pledged to unlock a further $100 billion per year from public and private sources until 2025 to assist emerging economies reduce carbon emissions. This will make the business case for new coal- and gas-fired power stations much weaker, and investment in alternative fuels development, such as hydrogen, much stronger.

The stimulus funding from the pandemic may be the opportunity the world needs in regard to keeping climate change in check. Countries that can look ahead and embrace the challenge while the funding is available can build export industries to provide their technology to the rest of the world. But climate change pressures won't be short-term, and the need for new technologies to address them will continue for most of this century at least.

Open innovation

The speed of innovation is accelerating and becoming more complex. Supply chains have internationalised and integrated. Interoperability and licensing between systems have become key to competitiveness. At the same time, AI, 3D printing and rapid prototyping, and virtual and augmented reality have put the capacity to innovate and develop new products in the hands and minds of more people than ever before. These advances, combined with global platforms, virtual models, and sensor networks that can create continuous flows of data to monitor dynamic environments – the artificial intelligence of things (AIoT) – means that the raw data available for responsive innovation is becoming increasingly fast and vast, and accessible to more people. Quantum computing – currently in development – will also usher in a new age of disruptive computer-processing power and speed.

My father used to tell me that 'ideas are cheap but getting them out is expensive'. Those cheap ideas can happen anywhere, but harvesting them and applying them in a way that leads to new products, services and profits is challenging and costly. A single person never achieves systems and product innovation and commercialisation alone, and due to the rapidity and global reach of modern knowledge systems, they are less likely to be achieved within a single organisation.

The theory of 'the firm', developed in 1937 by Ronald Coase, argued that firms exist when internalised transaction costs in a production process are cheaper than externalised services. For example, suppose it is cheaper and timelier to have legal services for a factory provided by a trained full-time employee than an external, independent legal firm. In that case, a person will be hired. The in-housing/ outsourcing adjustments, when managed well and balanced with the cost of bureaucracy, create firm boundaries and competitive units of human and other resources around production.

Coase's original case did not consider knowledge costs or profits, knowledge spillovers and transfers within firms, however, or the costs and benefits of embodied or tacit knowledge contained in their human workers. The 'profiting from innovation' theory, developed by David Teece in 1986, suggests contracting relationships and protection of a firm's intellectual property (IP) in supply chains is critical in generating profit for innovative firms, and this determines their market position and ability to exploit that IP over the longer term:

> Contracting for components or complements can reduce operating costs and risks, but it also entails strategic hazards. One of these is the risk of technology leakage (unintentional or otherwise) to competitors who are not part of the contract. A subtler hazard in such a relationship is the inability to pace or direct the evolution of a supplier's proprietary technology (Teece 2018, p. 1357).

Many organisations have turned to open innovation models to keep pace with or direct new and disruptive ideas coming from outside the firm. Open innovation models open an organisation up to greater collaboration, sharing and co-creating ideas in developing new innovations – sometimes with suppliers, customers and even competitors. It contrasts with 'closed innovation' models, where R&D operations are secretive, in-house ventures.

Open innovation was first explored as a modern business model by Harvard organisational theorist Henry Chesbrough in his 2003 book, *Open Innovation: The new imperative for creating and profiting from technology*. As Chesbrough explains:

> Open Innovation is based on the fundamental idea that useful knowledge is now widespread throughout society. No one organization has a monopoly on great ideas, and every

organization, no matter how effective internally, needs to engage deeply and extensively with external knowledge networks and communities. An organization that practices Open Innovation will utilize external ideas and technologies as a common practice in their own business (Chesbrough 2020).

Chesbrough's real contribution to open innovation, besides coining the term, is in demonstrating how his concept of open innovation can be applied and put into profitable operation. Chesbrough suggests a business is using an open innovation model when the use of external information is equal to the use of internal information. Open innovation models come in three main forms: inbound (acquiring knowledge in), outbound (selling, licensing or contributing knowledge out) and coupled (equal collaborative sharing), creating mutual benefits for the parties involved.

Open innovation models have been growing in popularity since Chesbrough first described them in 2003. Multinational companies like Procter & Gamble, Hewlett-Packard, Starbucks and Atlassian have all developed open innovation platforms or programs. An extensive survey of over 270 000 businesses across Europe found that inbound innovation models (where external knowledge is imported into the organisation) had increased in use between 2001 and 2008, with up to 93 per cent of businesses surveyed using inbound, open innovation business models (Fig. 7.6) (Cricelli *et al.* 2016).

Marco *et al.* (2015) also reviewed 10 years of literature on the performance of firms using open innovation models. They found that inbound and coupled open innovation between a company and its suppliers, research institutions or foreign-based organisations improved the performance of the organisation. In terms of policy implications, the authors suggest that publicly funded grants and R&D programs should focus on proposals that include teams with these three parties working together.

Actors within open innovation projects often function as knowledge brokers, and that much of the valuable knowledge shared

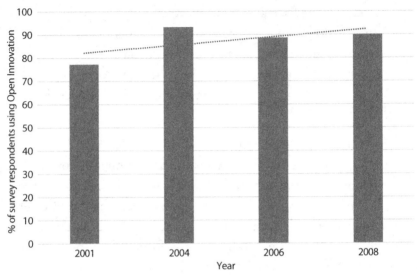

Fig. 7.6. Percentage of businesses using inbound open innovation models in the European Community Innovation Survey. Source: Cricelli *et al.* (2016).

in projects that use an open innovation model is tacit or human-embodied knowledge (often referred to as the 'know-how' and the 'know-who' – information that can't be codified or put into a computer) (Terhorst *et al.* 2018). Face-to-face interactions enabled by spatial proximity (say, in an industrial cluster) engender a greater sense of trust for the sharing of that tacit knowledge. It remains to be seen if better videoconferencing software and digital interaction spaces can replicate the transfer of tacit knowledge between open innovation partners as efficiently as interactions that perhaps mix social and professional engagement (meetings at a bar or club, events or recreational activities) (Terhorst *et al.* 2018; Terhorst pers. comm.).

With far greater power for individuals to contribute their ideas from anywhere in the world, and the processes of complex but continuous innovation increasingly requiring contributions from various knowledge domains, collaboration and groupthink have never been more critical or possible. These can and do lead to better technology and faster development.

Crowdsourcing for innovation

Wikipedia, Creative Commons, citizen science programs, hackathons and 'make-a-thons', chat-groups, YouTube, Reddit and many other platform-based communities of practice are all potential forums for crowdsourced innovation. These supplement real-life communities of practice, such as meet-up groups, clubs and associations, and professional industry groups. Journals and association publications are also crowdsourced, with quality control provided through peer review.

Many of these organisations and associations rely heavily on volunteer labour or free contributions, and people within them are often motivated by knowledge acquisition or a sense of community and purpose, rather than financial reward. Although they are incredibly important in knowledge transfer and, in particular, local knowledge transfer, they often suffer from sustainability issues if their business cases are not well supported or rely on the volunteerism or benevolent donations of a few individuals. Industry association groups sometimes levy members, but this can also deter membership. These digital and local crowdsourced knowledge platforms are currently not recognised or systemically funded in many countries in the same way as, say, local sporting groups or libraries.

Open-source software

'Open source' refers to computer coding that can be seen, shared and modified by users, compared to proprietary software, where the coding is hidden, controlled with permissions and can't be modified by users. Proprietary software is often packaged into products for sale (e.g. Microsoft Office packages, Google apps and Apple computer software are proprietary software). Proprietary software products have their IP and coding protected through patents or trademarks and can be vigorously defended in courts.

Open-source software is still licenced, and users have to accept the licence conditions, but the users are able to inspect and modify the coding, adapting it for purpose or improving on the original source code.

The big advantage of open-source software is that it evolves and improves faster than proprietary software. Coding bugs are fixed quickly, more efficient code is added by users and it can be modified for a range of applications. It is the gazelle of developing computer code. In 2018, 100 per cent of the world's top 500 supercomputers used open-source software. Today, most developmental R&D laboratories use open source, and much of the internet's architecture is built on open-source software (Prakash 2020). Cloud computing platforms such as ownCloud and Nextcloud are open source. The main operating system used for open-source development is Linux.

The organisation Opensource.com suggests that programmers use open source over proprietary software for five main reasons: control, training, security, stability and community.

The downside of open source is that it is open and therefore may not appeal as strongly to investors, venture capital managers or large buyers who want a competitive advantage through protected IP. This may include national defence forces and large private sector operators that seek an asymmetric knowledge advantage. Proprietary software has to be updated with patches to keep it secure so a firm needs to be of a certain size before it can start protecting its code and selling it as proprietary software. Registering trademarks and features of software or products (rather than the code itself) is often more practical for smaller businesses with unique digital products.

ArduPilot

ArduPilot is open-source software used in drone navigation. It helps drones navigate and move beyond the visual line of sight (BLVOS) of the controller, that is, on a form of autopilot.

The first version of ArduPilot was released in 2009 by Chris Anderson and Jordi Muñoz. Muñoz started building drones in his garage and got involved with the online group DIYDrones.com. He also focused on writing code and building drone parts. Muñoz took motion sensors from a Nintendo Wii remote and attached them to circuit boards to make a crude auto-navigation system. His partner in the venture, Chris Anderson, an influential journalist and editor of *Wired Magazine*, was so impressed with the posts Muñoz was putting on DIYDrones.com that he sent him $500 to buy parts and continue his work. Together they founded the company 3D Robotics and sold several prototype self-navigating drones (Morris 2015).

Fig. 7.7. Drone built by competitors in the Schools Section of the UAV Outback Challenge. Source: UAV Challenge.

The code used in ArduPilot, originally written by Muñoz, was open source. Over the next year it was completely rewritten by other members of the online group of enthusiasts who added functionality such as throttle control, mission scripting, sensor support, flight control and logging, and hardware optimisation.

By 2011, ArduPilot was being entered into autonomous copter competitions, and by October 2012 it had been taken up and further developed by drone hobbyists around the world. One of those hobby groups was the Australian group Canberra UAV, whose founding member, open-source developer Andrew Tridgell, further developed parts of the system and used it to enter the Australian UAV Outback Challenge. (A competitor drone in the UAV Outback Challenge can be seen in Fig. 7.7.) The ArduPilot team won sub-challenges in the UAV Outback Challenge in 2014 and 2016. The system moved onto a Linux board in 2014, and in October that year the 'Plane' code (a subset of the overall code) used in ArduPilot was successfully used in a drone search and rescue effort for a missing light plane in Florida.

In March 2016, 3D Robotics left the open-source team of ArduPilot, and the not-for-profit group ArduPilot.org was formed to continue its development. Since that time, ArduPilot has been continuously improved and used in drone navigation around the world. Notable achievements include:

- being featured in the Flirtey delivery drone in the Smithsonian Air and Space Museum
- being used in a drone flight over the North Pole
- being used in commercial drones, such as the SkyRocket
- being used in a range of equipment including agricultural tractors, submarines and aerial mapping.

Professor Jonathan Roberts, convenor of the UAV Outback Challenge, suggests that most drone companies use the ArduPilot navigation system because it is safer and performs better than much of the proprietary software available. The systems are continuously checked and tested by the community of drone coders around the world and it outcompetes most other navigation systems.

The developers who have worked on ArduPilot haven't received royalties from their code, but they have sold discrete products from the system and made gadgets and customised services for commercial products. The tagline for ArduPilot is 'Versatile, Trusted, Open'.

The original founders of ArduPilot, Jordi Muñoz and Chris Anderson, still own and run 3D Robotics (3DR), which is now one of the largest US-owned manufacturers of commercial drones (Morris 2015). 3DR now also sells drones to several clients, including the US Government and the US Department of Defense.

Summary

Innovation is being driven by new existential challenges to humankind, including climate change and pandemics. It is changing dramatically as a consequence of emerging digital technology and is becoming more open and collaborative. It is likely that the definition, measurement and geography of innovation will change substantially over the next decade. This will impact the ways in which innovative ventures can grow and be attracted to particular locations, and needs to be considered when attempting to build an innovation hotspot.

References

AI Rights Institute (2021) *Ideals and mission*. AI Rights Institute, San Francisco. <http://airights.net/ideals-and-mission/>

Australian Bureau of Statistics (2021) A year of COVID-19 and Australians work from home more. Australian Bureau of Statistics, Canberra, 17

March. <https://www.abs.gov.au/media-centre/media-releases/year-covid-19-and-australians-work-home-more>

Bojinov I, Choudhury P, Lane JN (2021) Virtual watercoolers: A field experiment on virtual synchronous interactions and performance of organizational newcomers. Working paper no. 21–125. Harvard Business School Technology & Operations Mgt Unit, Cambridge, Massachusetts. http://dx.doi.org/10.2139/ssrn.3855788

Broom D (2021) Home or office? Survey shows opinions about work after COVID-19. World Economic Forum, Cologny, Switzerland. <https://www.weforum.org/agenda/2021/07/back-to-office-or-work-from-home-survey>

Callaway E (2021) DeepMind's AI predicts structures for a vast trove of proteins. *Nature* **595**, 635–635. doi:10.1038/d41586-021-02025-4

Capo-McCormick L, Torres C, Benhamou M, Pogkoas D (2021) *The COVID-19 pandemic has added $19.5 trillion to global debt.* Bloomberg, New York. <https://www.bloomberg.com/graphics/2021-coronavirus-global-debt/>

Chesbrough HW (2020) *Open Innovation Results: Going beyond the hype and getting down to business.* Oxford University Press, Oxford, England.

Choudhury R (2020) Our work-from-anywhere future. *Harvard Business Review*, November–December. Cambridge, Massachusetts. < https://hbr.org/2020/11/our-work-from-anywhere-future>

Choudhury P, Crowston K, Dahlander L, Minervini MS, Raghuram S (2020) GitLab: work where you want, when you want. *Journal of Organization Design (Aarhus)* **9**, 23. doi:10.1186/s41469-020-00087-8

Cohn D (2020) *About a fifth of U.S. adults moved due to COVID-19 or know someone who did.* Pew Research Center, Washington DC. <https://www.pewresearch.org/fact-tank/2020/07/06/about-a-fifth-of-u-s-adults-moved-due-to-covid-19-or-know-someone-who-did/>

Coin360 (2021) Cryptocurrency Market Cap Charts. <https://coin360.com/charts/>

Coronavirus Research Center JHU (2021) *Vaccine research and development.* Johns Hopkins University, Baltimore. <https://coronavirus.jhu.edu/vaccines/timeline>

Council J (2021) VC firms have long backed AI. Now, they are using it. *Wall Street Journal*, 22 November. <https://www.wsj.com/articles/vc-firms-have-long-backed-ai-now-they-are-using-it-11616670000>

Cricelli L, Greco M, Grimaldi M (2016) Assessing the open Innovation trends by means of the Eurostat Community Innovation Survey. *International Journal of Innovation Management* **20**, 1650039. doi:10.1142/S1363919616500390

Ede B (2020) *Resetting our Future: Learning from tomorrow. Using strategic foresight to prepare for the next big disruption.* Changemaker Books, Hampshire UK.

Fleming E, Chilukuri S, Westra A (2017) *Digital in R&D: The $100 billion opportunity.* McKinsey & Company, New York, 1 December. <https://www.mckinsey.com/industries/life-sciences/our-insights/digital-in-r-and-d-the-100-billion-opportunity>

Hajkowicz S, Bratanova A, Schleiger E, Brosnan A (2020) Global trade and investment megatrends: Exploring opportunities and risks for the Australian economy during and after the COVID-19 crisis with strategic foresight. CSIRO Data61, Brisbane, Australia.

Hammer L (2018) *3D printing in construction, architecture and the built-environment.* 3D Printing Industry, London, 14 June. <https://3dprintingindustry.com/news/3d-printing-construction-architecture-built-environment-134530/>

International Energy Agency (2020) World Energy Outlook 2020. IEA, Paris.

IPBES (2019) Global assessment report on biodiversity and ecosystem services of the Intergovernmental Science-Policy Platform on Biodiversity and Ecosystem Services. (Eds ES Brondizio, J Settele, S Díaz and HT Ngo). IPBES secretariat, Bonn, Germany. doi:10.5281/zenodo.3831673

IPCC (2019) Climate change and land. An IPCC special report on climate change, desertification, land degradation, sustainable land management, food security and greenhouse gas flexes in terrestrial ecosystems.' United Nations, Geneva.

Johanson M (2021) The 'zoom towns' luring remote workers to rural enclaves. BBC, London, 9 June. <https://www.bbc.com/worklife/article/20210604-the-zoom-towns-luring-remote-workers-to-rural-enclaves>

Johns Hopkins University (2021) *COVID-19 Dashboard.* Center for Systems Science and Engineering (CSSE), Baltimore, Maryland. <https://publichealthupdate.com/jhu/>

King L (2020) 'The most significant climate legislation ever': How stimulus bill tackles warming planet. Arlington, US. USA Today Online, Arlington, Virginia, 27 December. <https://www.usatoday.com/story/news/politics/2020/12/27/covid-relief-legislation-includes-major-climate-change-provisions/4012433001/>

Lambrechts S (2016) Aldi's latest tech product is a 3D printer. techradar, Sydney, 12 February. <https://www.techradar.com/au/news/world-of-tech/aldi-s-latest-tech-product-is-a-3d-printer-1314822>

Laplume AO, Petersen B, Pearce JM (2016) Global value chains from a 3D printing perspective. *Journal of International Business Studies* 47, 595–609. doi:10.1057/jibs.2015.47

Loizos C (2021) As more artists and musicians turn their attention to NFTs, so, likely, do money launderers. TechCrunch, San Francisco, 25 March. <https://techcrunch.com/2021/03/24/nft_users/>

Marco G, Michele G, Livio C (2015) Open innovation actions and innovation performance. *European Journal of Innovation Management* **18**, 150–171. doi:10.1108/EJIM-07-2013-0074

Marshall A (1890) *The Principles of Economics*. Macmillan, London.

Matthews K (2018) 6 crypto crowdfunding platforms you need to know about. Born2Invest, London, 26 September. <https://born2invest.com/articles/6-crypto-crowdfunding-platforms-need-know/>

McCormack E (2020) *Theta (THETA) Guide: A decentralised video sharing platform*. Dchained LLC. <https://dchained.com/assets/theta-guide-decentralized-video-sharing-platform/>

Mordor Intelligence (2020) Crowdfunding market – growth, trends, COVID-19, impact and forecasts (2021–2016). Hyderabad, Telangana. <https://www.mordorintelligence.com/industry-reports/crowdfunding-market>

Morris R (2015) The Mexican immigrant who set up a global drone firm. BBC News, London, 23 February. <https://www.bbc.com/news/business-31356080>

Nature Climate Change (2021a) A year in the making. Editorial. *Nature Climate Change* **11**, 179. doi:10.1038/s41558-021-01010-z

Nature Climate Change (2021b) Enhancing commitments. Editorial. *Nature Climate Change* **11**, 457. doi:10.1038/s41558-021-01084-9

O'Halloran D, D'Souza F (2020) Data is the new gold. This how it can benefit everyone while harming no one. World Economic Forum, Cologny, Switzerland, 29 July. <https://www.weforum.org/agenda/2020/07/new-paradigm-business-data-digital-economy-benefits-privacy-digitalization/>

Palmer D (2021) Hollywood powerhouse CAA joins blockchain video network Theta. Coindesk, New York, 14 September. <https://www.coindesk.com/business/2021/05/27/hollywood-powerhouse-caa-joins-blockchain-video-network-theta/>

Pastor R (2020) 3D Printing lessons learned from COVID-19 (and how they will change manufacturing's future). *Industry Week*, 7 July. <https://www.industryweek.com/technology-and-iiot/additive/article/21136038/3d-printing-lessons-learned-from-covid19-and-how-they-will-change-manufacturings-future>

Pearce F (2016) What is causing the recent rise in methane emissions? *YaleEnvironment360*, 26 October <https://e360.yale.edu/features/methane_riddle_what_is_causing_the_rise_in_emissions>

Prakash A (2020) Linus runs on ALL of the top 500 supercomputers, again! *It's FOSS*, chmod777 Media Tech (OPC) Pvt Ltd, Uttar Pradesh, India. <https://itsfoss.com/linux-runs-top-supercomputers/>

Rayna T, Striukova L (2016) From rapid prototyping to home fabrication: how 3D printing is changing business model innovation. *Technological Forecasting and Social Change* **102**, 214–224. doi:10.1016/j.techfore.2015.07.023

Rimol M, Costello K (2021) Gartner says tech investors will prioritize data science and artificial intelligence about 'gut feel' for investment decisions by 2025. Gartner, Stamford, CT. <https://www.gartner.com/en/newsroom/press-releases/2021-03-10-gartner-says-tech-investors-will-prioritize-data-science-and-artificial-intelligence-above-gut-feel-for-investment-decisions-by-20250>

Rosalsky G (2020) Zoom towns and the new housing market for the 2 Americas. NPR – National Public Radio, Washington DC, 8 September. <https://www.npr.org/sections/money/2020/09/08/909680016/zoom-towns-and-the-new-housing-market-for-the-2-americas>

Schwab K (2020) The Great Reset Initiative: Now is the time for a 'great reset'. The World Economic Forum, Cologny, Switzerland, 3 June. <https://www.weforum.org/agenda/2020/06/now-is-the-time-for-a-great-reset/>

Service RF (2021) Huge protein structure database could transform biology. *Science* **373**, 478. doi:10.1126/science.373.6554.478

Skaff S, Day J, Pederson L, Nickerson A (2020) Artificial intelligence can't patent inventions: so what? IPWatchdog, Leesburg, Virginia, 13 July. <https://www.ipwatchdog.com/2020/07/13/artificial-intelligence-cant-patent-inventions/id=123226/>

Surae S (2018) The data-driven transformation in drug discovery. *Drug Discovery World*, London, 26 August. <https://www.ddw-online.com/the-data-driven-transformation-in-drug-discovery-784-201808/>

Tapscott R (2020) USPTO shoots down DABUS's bid for inventorship. IPWatchdog, Washington DC, 4 May. <https://www.ipwatchdog.com/2020/05/04/uspto-shoots-dabus-bid-inventorship/id=121284/>

Tapscott D, Tapscott A (2016) *Blockchain Revolution: How the technology behind Bitcoin is changing money, business, and the world*. Penguin, New York.

Technavio (2020) Global Crowdfunding Market 2021–2025. Research and Markets. Infiniti Research Limited, London. <https://www.researchandmarkets.com/reports/5031186/global-crowdfunding-market-2021-2025>

Teece DJ (2018) Profiting from innovation. In *The Palgrave Encyclopedia of Strategic Management*. (Eds M Augier and DJ Teece) pp. 1353–1358. Palgrave Macmillan UK, London.

Terhorst A, Lusher D, Bolton D, Elsum I, Wang P (2018) Tacit knowledge sharing in open innovation projects. *Project Management Journal* **49**, 5–19. doi:10.1177/8756972818781628

The Economist (2017) The world's most valuable resource is no longer oil, but data. *The Economist*, 6 May. <https://www.economist.com/leaders/2017/05/06/the-worlds-most-valuable-resource-is-no-longer-oil-but-data>.

The startups team (2018) Key crowdfunding statistics. Startups.com LLC, Columbus, Ohio, 3 December. <https://www.startups.com/library/expert-advice/key-crowdfunding-statistics>

Titley D (2017) Why is climate change's 2 degree Celsius of warming limit is so important? *The Conversation*, 23 August. <https://theconversation.com/why-is-climate-changes-2-degrees-celsius-of-warming-limit-so-important-82058>

IPBES (2019) Global assessment report on biodiversity and ecosystem services of the Intergovernmental Science-Policy Platform on Biodiversity and Ecosystem Services. (Eds ES Brondizio, J Settele, S Díaz and HT Ngo). IPBES secretariat, Bonn, Germany. doi:10.5281/zenodo.3831673

US Army Program Executive Office Soldier (2021) IVAS Production Contract Award. Media Release. Fort Belvoir VA, 31 March. <https://www.peosoldier.army.mil/News/Article-Display/Article/2556870/ivas-production-contract-award/>

World Health Organization (2021a) Coronavirus (COVID-19) Dashboard. WHO, Geneva. <https://covid19.who.int/>

World Health Organization (2021b) COVID-19 vaccine tracker and landscape. World Health Organization, Geneva. <https://www.who.int/publications/m/item/draft-landscape-of-covid-19-candidate-vaccines>

8

How to build an innovation hotspot

For the purposes of this book, an innovation hotspot has been defined as a town or city, state, precinct, or well-defined and -connected group of regional businesses, which can be seen to be growing and innovating disproportionately faster than its peers in the same country.

Building an innovation hotspot is essentially a place-based approach; the name 'hotspot' implies that it occurs in one place or jurisdiction. The hotspot may be a cluster of specialised industry, it may diversify or create new industry in a time of transition, or just improve overall productivity through innovation – depending on the forces driving change and the qualities of the existing industry structures.

Although it is a place-based approach, the actions to build a hotspot described in this final chapter won't necessarily be aimed directly at the place alone. They may be to modernise government or unlock finance. This book has sought to demonstrate that, in building a local innovative cluster or hotspot, sometimes there has to be an oblique and mixed approach – a focus on the technology, people and purpose, rather than just the place.

Is there a recipe?
During my winter studying at the Smithsonian Museum's Lemelson Center for the Study of Invention and Innovation in Washington DC in 2015–16, my initial talks with researchers focused on two questions:

1. What were the common elements of the six US innovation hotspots they had profiled as part of their 'Places of Invention' exhibition?
2. What was the role of government in their formation?

Despite my attempts to boil down history, the researchers at the Lemelson Center were adamant that there was no recipe for success for governments to apply. There was no list that they were willing to put together to say, 'This is how it is done.' They insisted that luck and historical context (serendipitous moves, incidental meetings, ideas over dinner and drinks, historical events and momentary inspiration) played a significant role in the early stages of the six hotspots in their exhibition (Molella and Karvellas 2015). Ultimately, they felt that an exact recipe for 'how to build an innovation hotspot' would be misleading and possibly unhelpful to government efforts and innovation policy.

After 25 years of being involved in and studying innovation policy and regional economic development, I can say that luck, context and history definitely play more than a significant part in whether a place suddenly tears away from the pack in terms of innovation and industry diversification. And while I also don't believe there is an exact recipe that fits every situation in time and place, there are some basic ingredients that need to be present for innovation to take off and new industries to be built. Similarly, the 'luck' involved in the development of successful innovation can be corralled. Otherwise innovation would occur randomly around the globe and there would be no definitive patterns or hotspots in the first place, meaning place and government policy wouldn't matter. But that is not the case.

More than just the innovation inputs

The Global Innovation Index (GII) lists innovation inputs as institutions, human capital and research, infrastructure, market sophistication, and business sophistication, and these each have two to three sub-measures (Cornell University *et al.* 2020), all of which can be seen in a range of innovation measures. But a 'recipe' to stimulate innovation requires more than just pouring in more innovation inputs, because although these are used to measure innovation, they don't describe actions a government can take to improve innovation.

A roadmap, on the other hand, is a set of sequential actions that applies to a particular situation. What I will attempt to describe in the next section are the basic ingredients for innovation based on the approaches of government, and some of the actions that can be mixed and matched to achieve higher levels of innovation, depending on the context. It is the rough method in the recipe section.

Context matters

Knowing the stage and capacity of the industry in a particular place is vital to knowing what innovation strategy to apply. In keeping with the baking analogy, Mr Ousmane Dione, the World Bank's then Country Director for Vietnam, stated in his speech to the International Development Innovation Association (IDIA) in 2019 that innovation policy was like making a soufflé. Heat needed to be applied at exactly the right time for the dish to rise and be successful. If you opened the oven too early, the soufflé would collapse and you would have wasted all the ingredients/resources that went into it. In his example, he was warning against investing too heavily in research and development (R&D) for new-to-the-world technology before the country had advanced closer to the technological frontier. In that context, Vietnamese industry needed to upskill and adopt technology created elsewhere (adoption and imitation phase to improve industrial productivity) before investing too heavily in the resource- and risk-intensive process of technological development (Dione 2019). Dione's advice follows the evidence that the greatest benefit from foreign direct investment (FDI) for many middle-income countries is gained through broad education provision and technology adoption, rather than creation (see Chapter 6). But new digital technologies are changing the costs and benefits of strategies all the time. Some countries now talk about 'leapfrogging' industrial steps with the latest digital technology.

The government actions that will best stimulate innovation will also differ depending on the industry. Parts of the digital sector are currently highly clustered and boosted by access to venture capital (VC), which is also highly clustered (see Chapter 6). But this is not the same for mining companies or the energy sector, which can be spread out, depending on the operations.

This book has outlined the evidence for six different, evidence-based approaches to innovation taken by governments over the last

50 years. As stated in the introduction, the various approaches overlap and have gone in and out of fashion, often following cycles of enthusiasm followed by disillusionment. This faddishness of innovation policy is rarely commented on, but like many other areas of society, innovation policymakers are definitely fashion followers. The latest trend appears to be mission-led innovation, and one aim of this book has been to let readers see this as part of a broader picture of what works and what doesn't work in innovation policy.

The basic ingredients

The basic ingredients for innovation have followed the approaches outlined in this book: skills, finance, culture, mission, technology and place (Fig. 8.1). To that we could also add infrastructure,

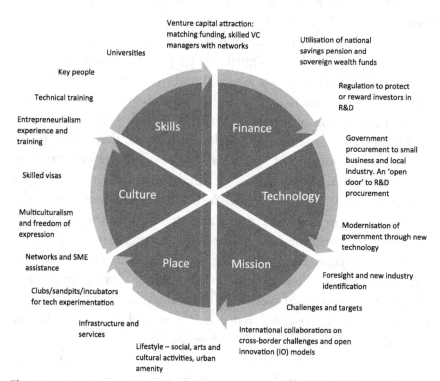

Fig. 8.1. Government actions to mix and match the basic ingredient to build an innovation hotspot.

particularly information and communications (ICT) infrastructure. Of those, there are two that are undoubtedly essential: skills and finance. In most circumstances if you mix those two together, you'll develop new processes and products – almost like reactive chemicals put into the same dish. The danger of concentrating on those two alone, however, is that the money may just be invested to create comfortable and secure lives, boost other markets, in particular the property market, or what some researchers have described as the FIRE sectors – finance, insurance and real-estate – the major features of a rent economy (Bezemer and Hudson 2016; Mazzucato 2019). This will ultimately lead to an uncompetitive local economy or wasteful innovation spending, and cause innovation efficiency to drop.

The mix of skills plus finance needs to be challenged or provided with a mission or purpose. New products and services must fulfil a need. Prior to 2009, New York City was full of talented and skilled people with access to finance, but it wasn't until the Global Financial Crisis in 2008–09 that a significant proportion of the workforce were released from their day jobs and had the incentive and time to build and commercialise the digital and financial products for the next generation of industry. Many New York City workers had been too time-poor to do that previously, but now their mission was to find new means of financial support. Entrepreneurialism sometimes increases in times of high unemployment (Plehn-Dujowich 2013), and the New York City government used the financial crisis in 2009 to create a new digital industry that is now second in the world in terms of attracting venture capital. Adapting to climate change and the race to a decarbonised economy, overcoming a pandemic with rapid vaccine development and creating new sources of wealth in the wake of a year of economic disruption are all missions that can inspire and incentivise future innovation.

So, is it skills, finance and purpose? That is a potent mix, but as Richard Florida and AnnaLee Saxenian demonstrate, culture, industrial structure and liveability (what Florida called 'the people climate') also play an important part in sustainable innovation over the longer term. A local social environment and industrial structure that encourages inclusivity, freedom of expression, tinkering, building and prototyping will attract and keep workers, create knowledge spillovers and provide informal training to its inhabitants that enable the economy to adapt to future challenges.

Developments in technology will force change and create opportunity. Seeing the potential of new technologies early and being a first mover in applying them to new problems will develop capability, create new products, improve productivity and push local industry into new sectors. Advancing and applying technology in the public sector can provide the finance and security needed by entrepreneurial startups to find their feet in a rapidly evolving environment. The bonus of using the public sector to develop new technology is that it can modernise and become more efficient at the same time. Government contracts based on developing new technology, such as radio, integrated circuits and the internet, built the foundations for the largest global hotspot in the world: Silicon Valley. We are now seeing the huge disruptive potential of a new wave of technologies – artificial intelligence, blockchain, augmented and virtual reality, global platforms, drones and robotics, 3D printing and additive manufacturing – and the early adopters, adapters, developers and deployers of these technologies will capture disproportionately more wealth.

Finally, place is important in the provision of infrastructure, urban amenity, regulation and stimulation. Place encourages the mix between social and professional lives – a mix that builds tacit knowledge and trusting creative partnerships and networks that build new enterprises. More and more, physical place will be supplemented with digital places, creating hybrid clusters and relationships.

The message of this book is that all the approaches listed above need to be considered in tailoring innovation strategy for a particular locale. No one approach on its own is likely to produce optimal results, but following a few basic principles can help mix these basic ingredients into an effective overall strategy.

Go with your strengths and look to the future

The first step in any effort to increase innovation in a region needs to start with examining existing industries and their future growth potential. A strategic foresight study can identify both existing industries with significant capability and emergent subsectors that can capitalise on large convergent long-term trends (often called megatrends), including the introduction of Industry 4.0 technologies. (Industry 4.0, or the Fourth Industrial Revolution, is a term used to denote the emerging phase of industrial production that will be will enabled by a new generation of primarily digital technologies. By this same token, Industry 1.0 was enabled by the steam engine, Industry 2.0 by electricity, and Industry 3.0 by computing technology.)

The OECD encourages centralised strategic foresight units within government to better anticipate change (thereby providing resilience and contingency disaster planning), encourage policy innovation and future-proof or stress-test strategy (OECD Strategic Foresight 2021).

My colleagues and I in the CSIRO Insight Team in Australia, in collaboration with university groups, are developing new methodologies to identify emerging industries and determine future growth potential. In most cases, future growth potential relies on a combination of existing capability and future need (Naughtin *et al*. 2021). Identification of future need is based on the large social, political, environmental, technological, economic and legal trends (megatrends) that will impact industries in the future. For example, the need to reduce carbon dioxide in the atmosphere and the political and legal changes that will regulate future carbon emissions will impact the future of fossil fuel industries and promote mining of other minerals such as lithium, silicon and rare earths.

The foresight methods we use in CSIRO integrate qualitative intelligence gathered through interviews and workshops with quantitative datasets related to individual businesses and industry groups. Foresight is about creating collective futures. Other groups around the world are building sophisticated predictive analytics tools to inform innovation policy. The World Economic Forum, for instance, has built the *Strategic Intelligence* platform to gather a range of datasets and analyse emerging dependencies that are likely to trigger change. This is to allow governments to anticipate change through the compilation of transformation maps (World Economic Forum 2021).

In most cases, new industries will evolve from an existing industry or area of regional advantage. A study of 70 Swedish regions over 30 years found that most new industries grew out of older industries and there was 'strong path dependency': 'Industries that were technologically related to the pre-existing industries in a region had a higher probability of entering that region than did industries that were technologically unrelated to the region's pre-existing industries' (Neffke *et al.* 2011).

Building completely new industries from scratch is possible, but riskier and usually more expensive. This is due to a lack of pre-existing supply chains, market knowledge, network advantage and local expertise. The development of new, digitally mediated knowledge networks (Reddit threads, YouTube channels, clubs and groups) may be dispersing the opportunity for new enterprises to be built, but knowing what enterprises will arise using these channels is not something governments can readily foresee. Instead, it is easier to wait until new businesses and enterprises form and then assist them to grow and scale up investment as they prove successful.

Go digital, global and encourage networked and open innovation

Digital technologies will both enable the evolution of existing industries and build new products that can become industries in themselves. Much of the new wealth being developed around the world, particularly in developed economies, is in the digital technology sector. For example, in the UK the digital technology sector grew six times faster than the rest of the economy in 2018 (Tech Nation 2020). In Australia, the technology sector has grown disproportionately faster than stocks on the Australian Stock Exchange (ASX) since 2017 (Hajkowicz *et al.* 2020). The digital technology sector was also significantly boosted by the COVID-19 pandemic with lockdowns and future infection controls likely to impact patterns and places of work into the future.

Investing heavily in applied digital capability – both training (schools, technical colleges and universities) and R&D – will improve existing operations and potentially create new products that can be applied elsewhere, thus contributing to exports. Most jurisdictions have STEM-skills courses, but these could be supplemented with incentives such as lower fee or free courses or be offered as essential components of other degrees or courses, such as a digital art, digital skills in history, digital design, farm robotics, cybersecurity in finance. Much of the workforce also needs to be re-educated to know the capabilities of new and emerging digital technologies and actively see new applications in their workplaces. Encouraging digital and data skills at work through tax deductions, retraining vouchers, and low-fee or free courses at public places such as libraries and in co-working centres will also provide more pathways for participation.

It is not enough just to train people in digital tech. There needs to be high-value local work, otherwise developers will quickly leave. The digital technology sector is relatively location-independent. That means it can quickly go off-shore when a local currency rises, or wages become too expensive. This happened to the digital games sector in Queensland, Australia, in 2008–2009, just before the global economic crises. The Queensland games sector had been nurtured with a large government-run industry fund that attracted international companies to set up in Brisbane. In 2008–2009, however, the large international games development companies suddenly closed their local studios as the Australian dollar rose to record levels against the US dollar. Within 2 years there were almost no international studios left. The ones that remained adapted to a new gaming environment (apps on mobile phones rather than large consoles), and were mostly home-grown companies that had international experience.

There is a global shortage of digital skills, and large digital companies are actively recruiting IT students before they graduate. The young and highly skilled are also the most mobile. Integrating digital technology students into local industry early in their training will assist them to grow local enterprises. Providing support and local networking will also help students develop new digital products that they can then commercialise. Commercialisation will require assistance with provision of advice regarding intellectual property (IP), legal protections and market development, but having co-developed products and services for a local need will ensure that the products have value in their application and have gone through initial testing.

The creation of an independent public VC fund that matches external funds will bring external investment into an ecosystem. But, more than the investment, it will bring in external expertise to assist young firms successfully commercialise their products. As discussed in Chapter 6, VC is highly concentrated, both geographically and in the types of businesses that it funds. It looks for highly scalable global products and breakthroughs: the next Airbnb, the next vaccine, the next energy storage technology. The US and China are the big consumer markets that VC targets, but it seeks technology to back from anywhere. In the past, VC has brought in talent, ideas and new enterprises to a particular location (e.g. Silicon Valley). VC managers have asked new enterprises to move within an easy distance to them to be funded, and this has been a critical component in maintaining and growing the existing digital clusters. But this might be changing in the post-COVID world; a world affected by infection controls, and the next wave of digital tech, including cryptocurrency, funding platforms and videoconference software. Embodied knowledge in individuals that is passed on through local face-to-face interactions is still powerful.

Encouraging international business links between the large technology markets and the local market will cultivate a global mindset. Overseas markets are scary for young enterprises, but they are important to engage with, especially for enterprises from smaller countries.

Part of the global market mindset is also learning alongside the best organisations and individuals around the world through open innovation models and open-source coding. Universities and other research training organisations have a vital role to play in forging links between local industry and international research and international markets. Universities also insulate a place from sudden downturns by providing retraining options in times of downturn or crisis. Going a step beyond enterprises practising open innovation, a whole region could practise an open innovation model and bring in as much knowledge as it exports.

This also means opening the doors to international students and skilled workers and creating a cosmopolitan intersection of cultures and ideas. Some of the most innovative places in the world (Hong Kong, Singapore, Shanghai and San Francisco) have blended different cultures and invested in different ways of thinking. There is a wealth of research to demonstrate that high performing teams are more likely to be diverse in culture, gender and ethnicity, although this may be more applicable to co-located teams than teams that are only connected via virtual networks (Wang *et al.* 2019).

Grow your own and go organic

This isn't about vegetables, this is about industry. Importing businesses is hard, expensive and often leads to growth without a lot of value added to the local economy.

Importing enterprises can be like attempting to grow a forest by transplanting one or two mature trees. They may take to the new conditions, but the risk that they don't is great and their impact if they do is very localised. But for the same price you can plant thousands of seeds. The trees that grow in their native soils are better adapted to local conditions, create stronger linkages with the other native flora and attract symbiotic organisms. Several papers have suggested that, just like trees in an emerging forest, it is more efficient and effective to grow your own industry rather than attract established ventures from outside (Chatterji *et al.* 2014).

Locating a business is a commercial decision that takes into account supply chains, infrastructure, markets, skills availability, establishment costs and future developments. Asking firms to co-locate in the development of a tech park or co-located cluster for the benefit of a single factor (a tax break or cheaper rent) often leads to disappointment or short-term development. If R&D laboratories in similar sectors are being set up then, yes, they may benefit from being near each other, having fit-for-purpose buildings and nearby facilities such as cafes and bars, and they can be great anchor tenants, but unless they are government research laboratories, then the decision on location is a commercial one that the enterprise itself should determine. Unless a government is prepared to subsidise a technology precinct heavily over the longer term, it is better to let an industry cluster develop organically. Build the cluster and attract industry by providing *the work* rather than *the place*. The businesses will cluster around work and opportunities in the places they can afford and operate best in.

Efforts should instead be focused on hothousing existing entrepreneurs emerging from local industry and from research and education institutions. The UK Catapult Network links nine centres across the UK that support local industry, innovative activity, foreign investment and global expertise. They bring together universities, local small and medium-sized enterprises (SMEs) and industry in a 'thirds' funding model (equal contributions from R&D funding, government grants and commercial enterprises). A 2021 review of the Catapult Network found:

> The Catapults support innovation through the provision of R&D infrastructure, specialist knowledge and expertise, partnership and collaboration building capabilities and business support. Since 2011, Catapults have directed over £2.5 billion of private and public sector investment to support innovators and advance the UK's economic capability in cutting-edge global markets. They have established over 2,000 academic collaborations, 14,750 industry collaborations and supported in excess of 8000 small and medium sized enterprises (SMEs) (Department of Business Energy and Industry Strategy 2021).

Attract key people

'Start with the people' is what the Honourable Paul Lucas, ex Minister for Innovation and the Information Economy in Queensland, told me: 'Good people will bring in other good people. They will be the magnet that will build the cluster.'

Attracting a whole enterprise and its workforce is difficult. Attracting individual people is easier, although the global competition for people who can build innovative enterprises is intensifying. People who have an international reputation in their field and a proven track record in building enterprises or valuable IP are incredibly important in building local innovation ecosystems. Individuals who can provide one-on-one mentoring to firms in their care through established networks can be critical. Local government may be able to leverage lifestyle, work, challenge, autonomy, status and opportunity to attract high-calibre people with good networks to other innovative groups.

Build industries through modernising government and creating regional challenges

Universities and government research institutions need R&D grants, but businesses, especially young businesses, need work contracts. Government spending in OECD countries is between 25–55 per cent of GDP (OECD 2020). Although most of this is spent directly on providing government services, the substantial government marketplace can also be a considerable source of funding for local innovation.

Government expenditure in OECD countries may also need to expand over the coming decades to cover the needs of aging populations, climate change adaptation and mitigation, recovery from COVID-19 and other pandemics, increased agricultural production and possibly higher education and training costs (Robinson 2020).

In addition to public expenditure on services and infrastructure, there are also growing funds invested in sovereign wealth funds (SWFs). Globally, over US$9 trillion was invested in SWFs in 2020 (see Chapter 6). Many SWFs have been established specifically for the future needs of an aging population and to assist in industry diversification in a decarbonised economy. Heavy investment by SWFs in domestic innovation to assist in these goals has not always been apparent.

Investing in innovative technology now will assist in both cutting the future servicing costs to government of aging populations, transitioning and diversifying the economy, adapting to climate change and building new local industry.

Government procurement has traditionally been very risk adverse – buying off-the-shelf products instead of spending on development and customisation. By being innovative itself and modernising through the development of new technologies through a two-way conversation with the research sector, governments can build their own local industries.

Schemes such as the small business innovation research (SBIR) in the US and the UK have very successfully opened a door to government departments and the government marketplace. Government departments participating in SBIR are asked to quarantine a percentage of their budget to dedicate to government contracts to R&D projects with small and innovative local businesses. Enterprises, including startups, are able to pitch new ideas and technologies they believe have government applications. Topping up SBIR schemes with income from SWFs or pension and superannuation funds would boost the finance available to government to transform and meet future challenges, as well as provide dedicated funding to build local industry with government contracts. Contracts that build collaborations between suppliers, contractors and global markets can build longer term networks and attract foreign expertise (Greco *et al.* 2015).

Regional challenges or missions provide direction for government spending on innovation and can also forge cross-sectorial partnerships between government, industry and the research sector (the 'triple helix' approach). Green challenges, energy targets and transformation goals, if designed well and implemented within set timeframes, can also attract further investment and talented people. To be successful, these challenges or missions need to reflect local priorities and be sufficiently funded over the timeframe needed to achieve the desired results (Roberts 2018).

VC packs a punch, but R&D is more evenly distributed. Encourage the triple helix model

The role of universities and research institutions in developing local innovation ecosystems cannot be overstated. Universities and research institutions bring in funding and expertise, build R&D infrastructure and provide pathways for immigrant entrepreneurs. Amornsiripanitch *et al.* (2021) found that 'Immigrant founders coming for education are likely to start their companies in the state in which they were educated, especially states where they received their graduate education, leading to potentially large local economic benefits'.

Importantly, universities also broker partnerships across sectors. The triple helix approach integrates government, industry and the research sectors in common regional goals (Etzkowitz 2008; Lee and Ngo 2012; Ricke *et al.* 2012). Some have added a fourth strand to this helix model: media and culture-based public participation (Peris-Ortiz *et al.* 2016), while others have also added in the natural environment as a fifth strand, especially in light of climate change (Carayannis *et al.* 2012).

Unlike venture capital, which is highly geographically concentrated, public R&D funding can be more widely distributed through local research organisations and innovative businesses. R&D tax credits have been found to efficiently incentivise higher levels of innovation, particularly product innovation in the SME sector (Hagel *et al.* 2013; Guceri and Liu 2019). Tax credits that incentivise partnerships with higher education institutions, government research groups and international organisations can also promote sustained innovation through the commercialisation of products and services.

Don't forget to have fun. Create the space to play

Innovation is about creative problem-solving, building new things, forming new relationships, growing enterprises and reputations, developing future visions and realising dreams. Supported and welcoming play and learning spaces can help people find their creative tribe, have fun, learn and bring their visions to life.

Creative play spaces could be libraries with technology learning spaces, incubators, meet-up groups, co-working centres, observatories, robotics and drones clubs, makerspaces, as well as legal instruments that give exemptions from certain legislation for experimentation (regulatory sandpits). Having aerospace and submarine facilities dedicated to playing with unmanned aerial vehicles (UAVs and drones) for enthusiasts to experiment with their technology without breaking the law is essential for development in these industries. Regulatory sandpits for the use of blockchain in financial services have been instrumental in trialling new technology for several emerging fintech firms.

Events for emerging technologies and industries are also important. Challenges and competitions such as hackathons, robot challenges, races, cybergames and AI art, for instance, can incentivise development through gaming. They attract young minds and stimulate them with a challenge and social connection. Integrating school teams with more professional groups in events provides two-way learning. This can create multiple entry points to the industry for anyone with the enthusiasm to get involved. The average age of a successful startup founder in the US in 2018 was 45, although this varied greatly by sector (Azoulay *et al.* 2018). Technology clubs allow experience from older club members to mix with enthusiasm and new perspectives offered by the young. For example, information on patents and protections can be passed down to younger members looking to commercialise their new ideas.

Sporting and recreation spaces, music venues, bars and restaurants, cultural and artistic institutions and social groups can be the overlay of enjoyment that will keep skilled people and foster the creative sharing of ideas and dreams for the future. Building the lifestyle attributes of a location is about more than just gentrification; it is about opportunity. To counter some of the negative attributes of gentrification – such as rapid property price rises and profiteering causing geographic inequality and pushing out people needing low-cost rental areas for both living and business – innovative property and sales taxes on development to fund infrastructure, transport and public spaces may need to be considered.

Virtual play spaces and swapping ideas are also part of the landscape and can allow significant peer-to-peer learning to supplement and bring new knowledge into the face-to-face forums.

If there was one common factor with the hotspots featured in the Lemelson Center's exhibition on 'Places of Invention', it was that the initial successful businesses were most often created by two founders. Many of the largest digital companies today also have two founders who worked on the initial business in a creative partnership: Apple was founded by Steve Jobs and Steve Wozniak, Google was founded by Larry Page and Sergey Brin, Microsoft was founded by Bill Gates and Paul Allen. An outlier, Facebook was developed by Mark Zuckerberg and four of his college dorm-mates – Eduardo Saverin, Dustin Moskovitz, Andrew McCollum and Chris Hughes.

All of these founders encountered each other in spaces outside formal classrooms where they could play and experiment with their technology and skills. Just like libraries and sporting associations, systemic support for technical play spaces and clubs needs to be considered as a part of an overall strategy to enhance regional innovation.

Expect it to take time

Building an innovation hotspot takes time. The faster hotspots (Estonia, East London Tech City and New York's digital sector) have arisen over two decades or so, but the largest in the world (Cambridge UK, San Francisco Bay area and Boston, US) have developed over centuries. It is unrealistic to expect elevated innovation outputs or the emergence of a high-tech cluster in a political term of 3–5 years. New technology takes years to develop, test, apply and commercialise, with differing timeframes depending on the technology and industry. Investment in innovation and new industries needs to be seen in longer timeframes, with funding relatively immune from political cycles. Evaluation frameworks for innovation funding need to be set to examine progress over decades, not years, and linked to detailed local business and industry data.

Summary

This book has offered a broad-brush overview of deliberate government approaches to enhance regional innovation or, in other words, to build an innovation hotspot. I have aimed to provide readers with the long view of the policy trends affecting the innovation field, so that a mature more comprehensive approach to innovation policy development can be taken and considered when being applied to a particular area.

I have described six broad areas of focus and evidence-based actions that have been used to enhance regional innovation: place, culture, skills, mission, finance and technology. Applying strategies is always contextual, however, so actions from these six broad areas will need to be mixed and matched depending on the existing capability of the industry, the type of industry, the availability of learning and education institutions, government expenditure and ability to leverage finance, social and cultural attributes of the region, available infrastructure and demographics.

The tricky thing about innovation is that the ways in which we innovate are always changing. Joseph Schumpeter's forces of creative destruction creating evolutionary shifts in technology and economics seem to be still very much apparent. So, what works today in innovation policy may not work into the future and will need to be constantly reassessed. The advice I have provided in the steps that leaders and decision-makers can take to build a hotspot is deliberately broad to allow future flexibility and the impacts of new technologies.

Over the next century, our societies and economies will face pandemics, climate change and aging populations. At the same time, we have an incredible range of new technologies that can assist us to innovate and collaborate in dramatically new ways. Artificial intelligence, blockchain, robotics and 3D manufacturing, augmented and virtual reality, and global cloud computing and sensor networks will change how we will live and work.

Unlocking finance, such as services spending, sovereign wealth funds and business investment, to apply these technologies and build the next generation of creative and skilled entrepreneurs will give us the best chance to not just survive but thrive in the next century.

Bringing it all together: Fort Collins, Colorado

Compiled with excerpts from Joyce Bedi, Senior Historian from the Lemelson Center at the Smithsonian National Museum of American History (Bedi 2015)

Over the last two decades, the university town of Fort Collins in Colorado, US, has emerged as a centre for:

clean energy and socially responsible innovation. In 2007, Fast Company listed Fort Collins as a 'fast city' that was 'generating patents at the rate of

11.45 a year per 10 000 people, nearly four times the U.S. city average'. Four years later, Wired Magazine cited Fort Collins as an 'emerging epicenter of high-tech industry'. The 2014 State New Economy Index, which ranks US states in the categories of knowledge jobs, globalisation, economic dynamism, the digital economy and innovation capacity, ranked Colorado 6th overall (Bedi 2015 referring to material from Park 2007, Davidson 2011, Information Technology and Innovation Foundation 2014).

It was the newest emerging region featured in the Smithsonian National Museum of American History's 'Places of Invention' exhibition in that opened 2015 (Molella and Karvellas 2015). The population of Fort Collins has tripled in the last 40 years.

How did a small, rural city like Fort Collins become an innovation hotspot? Government entities have always played a major role in development of Fort Collins. Fort Collins was first built in 1864 as a military settlement at the foot of the Rocky Mountains to protect the overland mail. An early federal government land grant program (the Morrill Act) established the Colorado Agricultural College in 1870, and this eventually evolved into the Colorado State University (CSU), in 1957. The Colorado-Big Thompson (CBT) River Project was built with federal reclamation funds between 1938 and 1956, and large federal agencies, including the Atomic Energy Commission, the National Bureau of Standards, and the National Center for Atmospheric Research, established laboratories or offices in Fort Collins or nearby Boulder in the 1950s.

As the 20th century progressed, agriculture faded as the most important segment of the Fort Collins economy. In 1970, a group of residents and local government officials created a committee that undertook foresight and planned for the year 2000.

The committee, Designing Tomorrow Today, reported projections for everything from housing and transportation needs to education, utilities and social services. A few years later, task forces related to the committee created a bullet point list of specific needs, among them constructing a new library, community center, river trail and park systems, as well as the less sexy but still necessary items such as new sewer lines and a land use plan. Locals were not standing by, either. About the same time, a trio of concerned citizens created a petition to create bicycle paths – a response to increasingly congested roads (Kendall 2018).

As Fort Collins' population continued to increase from the 1960s into the 1980s, the city's land development moved from farmland to suburban and urban use, reflecting the growth in non-agricultural ventures including manufacturing, retail, utilities, finance and services. Hewlett-Packard decided to open a small facility in the city in 1978. By the 1990s, historians Carl and Karen McWilliams argue, 'With one exception – Poudre Valley Hospital – Fort Collins' other top employers are all public-sector entities' (Fort Collins History Connection 2014).

Fort Collins in the 21st century – the move to clean energy innovation

In the 1990s, collaborative partnerships from the university, private industry and the city government started to come together in Fort Collins around the idea of clean energy (Bedi 2015). Local actors envisioned a 'triple helix approach' of the university working with local industry and utilising local energy infrastructure owned and operated by the City of Fort Collins Council.

Skills-led innovation – EECL

Most of the initial enthusiasm for green energy came from a newly appointed professor of mechanical engineering, Bryan Willson, who arrived at Colorado State University in 1988. Willson gained permission and a lease from the City of Fort Collins Council to convert an abandoned municipal power plant to the new Colorado State University Engines and Energy Conversion Laboratory (EECL), which opened in 1992.

Willson and his colleagues at EECL researched:

> new technologies ranging from green building, cleaner methods of oil and gas production, algae-based biofuels, smart grid power distribution systems and energy technology for the developing world … By the 2010s, the EECL was partnering with the Colorado Clean Energy Cluster [and also cultivating] strong relationships with the City of Fort Collins, the Colorado Energy Office and many other local, state and national groups whose focus was on sustainability and clean energy (Bedi 2015).

Willson's laboratory and students worked with local industry to research energy applications and patent new technology (Colorado Clean Energy Cluster 2016).

Mission-led innovation – FortZED

In 2008, a mission was developed to direct local innovation towards clean energy, long before the rest of the world began setting zero-emission targets. FortZED was created and EECL was a founding member (Energy Institute 2021).

> FortZED is a collaboration of Colorado State University, the city of Fort Collins, and local clean technology companies, with the goal of creating a 'zero-energy district,' that is, a district that produces at least as much energy as it uses … The project seeks to be a model that can be replicated

elsewhere for using existing electrical grids to achieve energy sufficiency (Bedi 2015).

Technology-led innovation – Spirae Inc. and InteGrid

FortZED works on a smart grid technology developed by local startup company Spirae Inc. The zero energy target utilised a new locally developed smart grid, which made it possible to measure and develop clean energy sources. The grid integrates:

renewable and distributed energy sources and produces a more reliable electricity supply by being responsive to energy supply and use ... Active management of multiple energy resources, both traditional and renewable, and two-way communication with consumers ... allows adjustments to energy needs and, in some cases, feeds unused energy back into the grid. Spirae's goal was to achieve this while working within existing utility infrastructures (Bedi 2015).

The InteGrid Laboratory, a collaboration between Spirae and CSU, was established in 2006 within the CSU Engines and Energy Conversion Laboratory to test the feasibility of the system by simulating an electrical grid using a whole-of-energy inputs (renewable, conventional, residential, commercial) approach. By doing so they created and tested a micro-grid capable of distributed power – a starting point for FortZED (Bedi 2015).

A $6.3 million grant from the US Department of Energy with a nearly equal amount of community support funded the RDSI [Renewable and Distributed Systems Integration] project and 'jump started FortZED by testing out a number of technologies that reduce peak energy use and integrate renewable energy, such as solar panels, into the district's electric energy system.' ... The participation of the city and the local utility company, and especially their leaders' willingness to try new things, was crucial to the success of the RDSI project (Bedi 2015; FortZED 2014).

The program ended in 2017 after a majority of its projects were completed. While FortZED and the RDSI study were the largest and most visible manifestations of government support of clean energy research in Fort Collins, there are other examples. For example, inventor Ed VanDyne and his company VanDyne SuperTurbo, which is building a new kind of turbocharger that is connected to a continuously variable transmission, have received significant support from the federal Small Business Innovation Research Program. Inventor Amy Prieto's work centres on inventing a rechargeable battery that will last longer, charge faster and is free of toxic materials (Bedi 2015). She and her company Prieto Battery have been supported by the Colorado state government Office of Economic Development and International Trade. The US

Department of Energy has supported the EECL, and appointed Bryan Willson as a program director at the Advanced Research Projects Agency–Energy (ARPA-E) (Bedi 2015).

Culture-led innovation – Fort Collins Urban Renewal Authority
Being at the foot of the Rocky Mountains, Fort Collins markets itself as a destination for those seeking outdoors recreation such as mountain biking, hiking, fishing and kayaking, as well as arts and cultural pursuits such as live theatre, art and museums and music festivals. It also claims to be North America's capital for craft beer, with over 20 breweries, which produce 7 per cent of craft beer in the US (Visit Fort Collins 2020). Some have suggested that knowledge workers migrate to Fort Collins for the 'beer, bands, and bikes' (Bedi 2015) (Fig. 8.2).

Urban planning and renewal has also had a long history in Fort Collins. City planning became a major concern in the 1980s, when city planners sought to limit urban sprawl and revitalise historic inner-town precincts, including the 'Old Town'. They also sought to allow denser populations where amenities existed, such as around shopping centres, parks, employment centres, schools and childcare (Fort Collins Museum and Discovery Science Center 1996). A sales tax on new property was introduced in 1992 to fund and maintain green zones around the city and limit growth to certain areas. In 2018, it generated $14 million, which was directed into conserving nearly 18 000 hectares of open space and recreational facilities.

Fig. 8.2. Downtown Fort Collins, Colorado. Licenced under CC BY 3.0 by Citycommunications at English Wikipedia.

The Fort Collins Urban Renewal Authority today runs redevelopment and renewal projects in both downtown and outer suburbs prone to urban 'blight' or degradation over time. They have identified blighted brown- and greyfields areas and marked them as Urban Renewal Plan Areas to redevelop. This redevelopment aims to provide more housing, reduce crime, provide infrastructure, reactivate and preserve historic buildings, and improve pedestrian, bike and transport connectivity. The aim is to boost local jobs, investment, new businesses and economic value (Fort Collins Urban Renewal Authority 2020). The city also supports infill and redevelopment to meet climate action strategies and other community goals.

Finance-led innovation – now new venture capital firms are setting up in Fort Collins
According to Engineering Professor Bryan Willson, 'The money trails innovation in our ecosystem' (Willson 2021, *pers. comm.*). The university-based companies and startups often use R&D funding and then transition to 'boot-camp' programs run through the university-based Research to Markets (R2M) Office. Many of the new enterprises are able to launch, grow and exit without accessing dilutive funding by using the support of the university. External funding programs also work with the National Renewable Energy Laboratory system that supports the clean energy cluster in Fort Collins. Donors to National Renewable Energy Laboratory include the US bank Wells Fargo as well as well-known US philanthropists and wealthy individuals.

Over the last twenty years a small number of incubators and VC firms have established a presence in the city. These include non-profits associated with Colorado State University (Innosphere and CSU Institute of Entrepreneurship linked to CSU Ventures) and new private companies (i2B Capital, Vet DC, and Factor[e]). A joint program called REACH (Rockies/Plains Energy Accelerator for Commercializing Hardtech) hopes to extend 'The Fort Collins Model' to 12 surrounding states.

Willson says that private VC has played only a minor role in building the cluster. 'I think 10 years back it was pretty small, US$1 million to US$2 million.' When asked if VC was a factor in attracting entrepreneurs to the city, Willson suggests 'It's a visible thing that convinces people we have a vibrant VC community, but only a small number of our ventures ever seek or receive VC funding.'

The City of Fort Collins City Plan also states that it is actively seeking to assist local institutions in attracting more R&D and investment into entrepreneurial activities:

Support and invest in the expansion of research and development institutions, business incubators, entrepreneurial networks, business development programs and other physical assets necessary to support entrepreneurship. These assets should also include financial tools and capital to support innovation and entrepreneurship by leveraging local, state and national grant programs and lending tools. Continue and grow partnerships with CSU and other institutions to identify research activities and associated needs that can be leveraged into business creation (City of Fort Collins 2021).

Place-led innovation – targeted industries and clusters

Place-led innovation efforts to co-locate industry seem to have received the least investment in Fort Collins, as the whole city itself is small enough for 'big city ideas and small town relationships' (City of Fort Collins 2020). The city has selected certain industries to target, however, and in some cases provided funding to bring large manufacturers to the city.

In 2016, the city provided $40 million in tax incentives and fee waivers to attract the headquarters of Woodward, a designer and manufacturer of energy and aerospace products. This fits with the city's emphasis on green energy technologies, but the expenditure has been criticised, with critics suggesting that jobs at Woodward weren't filled by locals; people were imported and therefore it only supported growth, not new jobs (Kendall 2018).

Prioritised sectors in Fort Collins planning include biosciences, software and hardware and water innovation, as well as more general clusters based around those industries that are unique to Fort Collins, including breweries and the creative arts. There appears to be natural clustering around facilities and precincts, with creative arts businesses around the downtown theatres and venues, and biosciences around the university facilities. These have been actively facilitated through zoning and city planning.

In 2009, Harmony Tech Park was initiated, covering 42 hectares on the outskirts of town. Progress in filling the technology park appears to have been slow however, with approximately US$7 million in infrastructure installed, 16 of the 42 hectares sold and only 10 developments completed or underway in 2020 (Harmony Technology Park 2021).

Rapid growth in Fort Collins

The population of Fort Collins has grown rapidly since the early 1960s, and this has caused growing pains. There have been increases in downtown traffic congestion and property prices, impacts on the local environment, and complaints from longer-terms locals that they no longer feel connected or identify with what they perceived to be a never-ending sprawling metropolitan area (Kendall 2018).

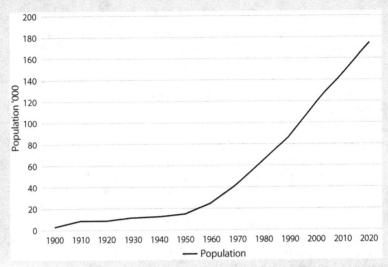

Fig. 8.3. Population growth in Fort Collins, Colorado 1900–2020. Source: World Population Review.

Fort Collins is still growing at 2 per cent per year, outpacing the growth of the surrounding area and the Colorado state average (Fig. 8.3).

A customised approach for world advantage
It is not an accident that Fort Collins has emerged as a hotspot of invention and innovation.

> *Active members of the university, city and local business community, with support from local, state and federal governments, pursue collaborations that further research and development on an array of sustainability issues. The mountains, Cache de la Poudre River, agricultural fields, university campus and historic downtown with its coffee shops and pubs all added to the sense of community, common history and environmental responsibility (Bedi 2015).*

Fort Collins also actively combined innovation strategies, was forward-thinking in terms of utilisation of new technologies for future goals and leveraged its geographic and historical advantages to attract talented people, investment and innovative businesses.

Overall, this successfully boosted the economy and grew unique and world-leading new industries. No transformation occurs without a degree of disruption, but Fort Collins is an example of customised approaches to innovation and new industry creation that has created a growth centre in a small town of America.

References

Amornsiripanitch N, Gompers PA, Hu G, Vasudevan K (2021) Getting schooled: the role of universities in attracting immigrant entrepreneurs. Working paper 28773. National Bureau of Economic Research, Cambridge, Massachusetts.

Azoulay P, Jones B, Kim D, Miranda J (2018) Research: The average age of a successful start-up founder is 45. *Harvard Business Review*, Boston, Massachusetts, 11 July. <https://hbr.org/2018/07/research-the-average-age-of-a-successful-startup-founder-is-45>

Bedi J (2015) Fort Collins: Campus and city combine their energies for a greener planet. In *Places of Invention*. (Eds A Molella, A Karvellas) pp. 180–210. Smithsonian Institution Scholarly Press, Washington DC.

Bezemer D, Hudson M (2016) Finance is not the economy: reviving the conceptual distinction. *Journal of Economic Issues* **50**, 745–768. doi:10.1080/00213624.2016.1210384

Carayannis EG, Barth TD, Campbell DFJ (2012) The Quintuple Helix innovation model: global warming as a challenge and driver for innovation. *Journal of Innovation and Entrepreneurship* **1**, 1–12. doi:10.1186/2192-5372-1-2

Chatterji A, Glaeser E, Kerr W (2014) Clusters of entrepreneurship and innovation. *Innovation Policy and the Economy* **14**, 129–166. doi:10.1086/674023

City of Fort Collins (2020) *Business: Target industries.* City of Fort Collins, Colorado. <https://www.fcgov.com/business/target-industries>

City of Fort Collins (2021) *City Plan: Economic health. EH 2.2 – Assets to Support Entrepreneurship.* City of Fort Collins, Colorado. <https://www.fcgov.com/cityplan/economic-health-policies>

Colorado Clean Energy Cluster (2016) About the CCEC. Colorado Clean Energy Cluster. <http://www.coloradocleanenergy.com/about>

Cornell University, INSEAD, WIPO (2020) *The Global Innovation Index 2020: Who will finance innovation?* (Eds S Dutta, B Lanvin, S Wunsch-Vincent) Cornell University, INSEAD, WIPO, Ithaca, Fountainebleau, Geneva.

Davidson A (2011) The emerging epicenters. *Wired* **19**, 130.

Department of Business Energy and Industry Strategy (2021) Catapult Network Review: How the UK's Catapults can strengthen research and development capacity. BEIS Research Paper Number 2021/013. UK Government, London.

Dione O (2019) *Opening remarks.* International Development Innovation Association, Hanoi, 15 May. IDIA. <https://www.idiainnovation.org/keynote-address-idia-principal-remarks>

Energy Institute (2021) Bryan Willson, Colorado State University, Fort Collins. <https://energy.colostate.edu/willson/>

Etzkowitz H (2008) *The Triple Helix: University–Industry–Government Innovation in Action.* Routledge, Milton Park, Oxfordshire.

Fort Collins History Connection (2014) Fort Collins History and Architecture, Table I, Fort Collins Population Trends, 1880–2010. <https://history.poudrelibraries.org/contexts/table1>

Fort Collins Museum and Discovery Science Centet (1996) *Fort Collins Timeline 1980; Local History Archive.* Fort Collins Museum, Fort Collins, Colorado. <https://history.fcgov.com/timeline/index.php>

Fort Collins Urban Renewal Authority (2020) *About the URA.* Fort Collins, Colorado. <https://www.renewfortcollins.com/about-the-ura/>

FortZED (2014) RDSI, FortZed's Jump Start Phase I and II. <http://fortzed.com/what-is-fortzed/smart-projects>

Greco M, Grimaldi M, Cricelli L (2015) Open innovation actions and innovation performance: a literature review of European empirical evidence. *European Journal of Innovation Management* **18**, 150–171. doi:10.1108/EJIM-07-2013-0074

Guceri I, Liu L (2019) Effectiveness of fiscal incentives for R&D: quasi-experimental evidence. *American Economic Journal: Economic Policy* **11**, 266–291. doi:10.1257/pol.20170403

Hagel J, Seely Brown J, Samoylova T, Lui M (2013) From exponential technologies to exponential innovation. Report 2 of the 2013 Shift Index series. Deloitte, New York.

Hajkowicz S, Bratanova A, Schleiger E, Brosnan A (2020) Global trade and investment megatrends: Exploring opportunities and risks for the Australian economy during and after the COVID-19 crisis with strategic foresight. CSIRO Data61, Brisbane, Australia. <https://www.csiro.au/en/research/technology-space/data/Data-driven-insights>

Harmony Technology Park (2021) Harmony Technology Park: sales and information. MAVD Projects, Ann Arbor, Michigan. <http://harmonytechnologypark.com/>

Information Technology and Innovation Foundation (2014) *The 2014 State New Economy Index: Benchmarking Economic Transformation in the States.* Information Technology and Innovation Foundation, Washington, DC.

Kendall L (2018) Did Fort Collins grow too big too fast? The Colorado city's unwieldy expansion offers a cautionary tale for similar Western locales. *High Country News*, Paonla, Colorado, 28 March. <https://www.hcn.org/articles/the-montana-gap-has-fort-collins-grown-too-big-too-fast>

Lee SJ, Ngo TH (2012) Riccardo Viale and Henry Etzkowitz: the capitalization of knowledge: a triple helix of university–industry–government. *Higher Education* **63**, 161–163. doi:10.1007/s10734-011-9427-x

Mazzucato M (2019) *What is economic value, and who creates it.* TED Ideas worth spreading. New York. <https://www.ted.com/talks/mariana_mazzucato_what_is_economic_value_and_who_creates_it>

Molella AP, Karvellas A (2015) *Places of Invention*. Smithsonian Institution Scholarly Press, Washington DC.

Naughtin C, Moyle C, Pandey V, Renando C, Poruschi L, Torres de Oliveira R, Doan N, Schleiger E (2021) *A new chapter: Opportunities to seed new industries for Queensland over the coming decade*. CSIRO and the Queensland University of Technology, Brisbane.

Neffke F, Henning M, Boschma R (2011) How do regions diversify over time? Industry relatedness and the development of new growth paths in regions. *Economic Geography* **87**, 237–265. doi:10.1111/j.1944-8287.2011.01121.x

OECD (2020) *General government spending as a proportion of GDP*. OECD Data, Paris. <https://data.oecd.org/gga/general-government-spending.htm>

OECD Strategic Foresight (2021) *What is strategic foresight?* OECD, Paris. <https://www.oecd.org/strategic-foresight/whatisforesight/>

Park A (2007) Fast Cities 2007: from Chicago to Shanghai, urban centers that are shaping our future. *Fast Company*, 1 July, New York. <https://www.fastcompany.com/59941/fast-cities-2007>

Peris-Ortiz M, Ferreira JJ, Farinha L, Fernandes NO (2016) *Multiple Helix Ecosystems for Sustainable Competitiveness*. Springer, Cham, Switzerland.

Plehn-Dujowich JM (2013) The dynamic relationship between entrepreneurship, unemployment, and growth: Evidence from U.S. industries. In *Topics in Entrepreneurship*. (Ed. B Cardenas) pp. 1–32. Nova Science Publishers, Hauppauge, New York.

Ricke A, Laestadius S, Etzkowitz H (2012) *Innovation Governance in an Open Economy: Shaping regional nodes in a globalized world*. Routledge, Oxford.

Roberts A (2018) *Innovation Facets Part 4: Mission-oriented innovation*. OECD Observatory for Public Sector Innovation, Paris.

Robinson M (2020) *Bigger Government: The Future of government expenditure in advanced economies*. Arolla Press, Switzerland.

Tech Nation (2020) UK tech for a changing world. Tech Nation Report 2020. London. <https://technation.io/report2020/>

Visit Fort Collins Council (2020) *About Fort Collins*. Visit Fort Collins Colorado. <https://www.visitftcollins.com/maps-info/about-fort-collins/>

Wang J, Cheng GHL, Chen T, Leung K (2019) Team creativity/innovation in culturally diverse teams: a meta-analysis. *Journal of Organizational Behavior* **40**, 693–708. doi:10.1002/job.2362

World Economic Forum (2021) *Strategic Intelligence: Strategic insights and contextual intelligence*. World Economic Forum, Cologny, Switzerland. <https://intelligence.weforum.org/>

Index

Printed in the United States
by Baker & Taylor Publisher Services